OFFICIAL CROCHET
AMIGURUMI

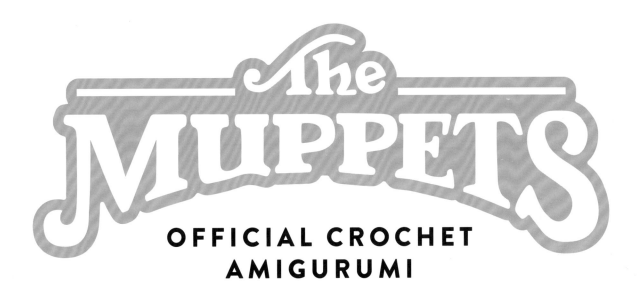

OFFICIAL CROCHET AMIGURUMI

16 Projects to Create Your Favorite Muppets

DREW HILL

weldonowen

For Mumpkin and Dad, thank you
for introducing me to The Muppets
and many other things that sparked
my creativity—I love you both.

CONTENTS

LETTER FROM SAM

Greetings, my fellow crocheters,

It is I, Sam Eagle. Few know of my fondness for handicrafts, but I love crochet almost as much as I love this great nation I call home. And even though my fellow Americans didn't invent this beloved art form, I believe in my heart that it is distinctly patriotic. If Betsy Ross could have crocheted the first flag for our young country, I think she would have. Because what is more American than joining the many through strategy, and by hooking loops in a continuous chain until they create a perfect union. That is why I am so delighted that you hold in your hands this very book. Because now, The Muppets can be associated with fine, upstanding skills such as the half-double crochet stitch, the magic ring, and ... *the picot*. Not any of their usual nonsense like doing cannonballs into pools of tapioca pudding or tap-dancing in oatmeal.

Whatever country you call home, and whatever Muppet you feel best personifies you, I hope you find great enjoyment in your crochet. And should your answers to those questions be the United States and Sam Eagle, then you have my additional gratitude.

Best of luck in your crochet endeavors,

INTRODUCTION

The Muppets were a staple in my household growing up. I have always loved the quirky, hilarious, and lovable cast of characters. Whether being featured in their own original stories or bringing classic works like Robert Louis Stevenson's *Treasure Island* to life, The Muppets have never failed to delight. From my first introduction, I was inspired by the design and craftmanship that so clearly went into the creation of these iconic characters. The vibrant color palette and the delightful use of texture and scale set my creative mind buzzing.

My grandma taught me to knit when I was ten—yarn has since been a steady part of my life right alongside The Muppets. At seventeen, I taught myself to crochet, but it wasn't until I discovered amigurumi that I was well and truly hooked (pun absolutely intended). The word *amigurumi* is a Japanese portmanteau of *ami* ("to knit or crochet") and *nuigurumi* ("stuffed doll/toy"). My creative mind, still buzzing, went to work designing and making them right away. I haven't stopped since.

Combining these passions to turn The Muppets into amigurumi has been both a dream come true and a challenge. The patterns in this book are perfect for seasoned crocheters or advanced beginners who are looking for a challenge.

Now it's time to grab some yarn and a hook, put on your favorite Muppets movie or show, and bring these beloved characters to life!

THE STARS
OF THE SHOW!

Kermit the Frog!

Kermit may be the world's most famous amphibian, but he has never let his international success go to his head or his flippers. Under his iconic green exterior, Kermit is still a lovable every-frog, a tadpole from a small-town swamp who got lucky and made it big in showbiz. Kermit's main role is as leader of The Muppets, trying to keep the show going and the craziness under control. It's not an easy job, but he loves everything about it. The Muppets are his colleagues, his friends, his family.

FUN FACT Kermit made his first on-screen appearance on a local television series back in 1955. Back then, instead of being green, this frog was seen in black and white!

Kermit the Frog

FINISHED MEASUREMENTS
Height: 8 in. / 20 cm
Width: 2.5 in. / 6.5 cm

YARN
Worsted weight (#4 medium) yarn, shown in Big Twist *Value* (100% acrylic, 380 yd. / 347 m per 6 oz. / 170 g skein)
Skin: Light Green
Mouth: Varsity Red
Eyes: White
Eyes: Black

Worsted weight (#4 medium) yarn, shown in Loops & Threads *Impeccable* (100% acrylic, 285 yd. / 260 m per 4.5 oz. / 127.5 g skein)
Collar: Citron

HOOK
US F-5 / 3.75 mm hook

NOTIONS
- Pink felt for tongue
- Polyester stuffing
- Tapestry needle
- Hot glue gun
- Removable stitch markers

GAUGE
Gauge is not critical for this project. Ensure your stitches are tight so the stuffing won't show through.

SPECIAL STITCHES
Picot (picot): Ch 3, sc into the back bump of first ch made
Back Loop Only (BLO): Work through back loop only.

NOTE
The mouth and head are separate pieces that get crocheted together, so it is important to make them in order.

For more information on how to make Kermit, including tips, step-by-step pictures, and videos, scan this QR code!

MOUTH

With Varsity Red, make a magic ring

Rnd 1. Sc 8 in ring [8]

Rnd 2. (Inc, sc, sc 3 in the same st, sc) x2 [14]

Rnd 3. (Inc, sc 3, sc 3 in the same st, sc 2) x2 [20]

Rnd 4. Sc, inc, sc 4, sc 3 in the same st, sc 4, inc, sc 4, sc 3 in the same st, sc 3 [26]

Rnd 5. Sc, inc, sc 6, sc 3 in the same st, sc 6, inc, sc *place a stitch marker in the last st made*, sc 4, sc 3 in the same st, sc 4 [32]

Fasten off the yarn and set aside for now.

ARMS (Make 1 Right and 1 Left)

With Light Green, make a magic ring

Rnd 1. Sc 8 in ring [8]

Rnd 2. *Right Arm:* In FLO sl st, ch 3, starting in the second ch from the hook sl st 2, sl st 2 on the ring, (ch 4, starting in the second ch from the hook sl st 3, ch 4, starting in the second ch from the hook sl st 3, sl st on the ring) x2, through both loops sc 4 [8 st with 5 fingers]
Left Arm: In FLO sl st, (ch 4, starting in the second ch from the hook sl st 3, ch 4, starting in the second ch from the hook sl st 3, sl st on the ring) x2, sl st, ch 3, starting in the second ch from the hook sl st 2, sl st 2 on the ring, through both loops sc 4 [8 st with 5 fingers]

Rnd 3. In BLO (using the back loops from rnd 2) sc 4, through both loops sc 4 [8]

Rnd 4. (Sc 2, dec) x2 [6]

Rnds 5–14. Sc in each st around, *after a few rnds, add a small amount of stuffing to the hands only* [10 rnds of 6 st]

Rnd 15. Press the previous rnd together so the st line up and sc them together [3]

Fasten off the yarn and weave in the ends.

HEAD AND BODY

With Light Green, make a magic ring

Rnd 1. Sc 8 in ring [8]

Rnd 2. (Inc, sc, sc 3 in the same st, sc) x2 [14]

Rnd 3. Sc in each st around [14]

Rnd 4. (Inc, sc 3, sc 3 in the same st, sc 2) x2 [20]

Rnd 5. Sc in each st around [20]

Rnd 6. Sc, inc, sc 4, sc 3 in the same st, sc 4, inc, sc 4, sc 3 in the same st, sc 3 [26]

Rnd 7. Sc in each st around [26]

Rnd 8. Sc, inc, sc 6, sc 3 in the same st, sc 6, inc, sc 5, sc 3 in the same st, sc 4 [32]

Rnd 9. Sc, *grab the Mouth and line it up, wrong sides together, so the next Light Green st lines up with the st that was marked on rnd 5 of the Mouth. Insert hook through both the Light Green and Varsity Red st and crochet them together* sc 8, inc, ch 1, inc, sc 8, *work the rest of the rnd in only the Light Green st* inc, sc 13 [34]

Rnd 10. Sc, *work into the Varsity Red st on the bottom half of the mouth* sc 6, (inc) x2, sc 6, *work the rest of the rnd in the Light Green st* sc 13 [30]

Rnd 11. Sc, sc BLO 16, sc 13 [30]

Rnd 12. (Sc 3, dec) x6 [24]

Begin stuffing the Head—add just enough stuffing so that the Head keeps its shape without causing the Mouth to bulge:

Rnd 13. (Sc 2, dec) x6 [18]

Rnds 14–17. Sc in each st around [4 rnds of 18 st]

Rnd 18. (Sc 2, inc) x6 [24]

Rnd 19. (Sc 3, inc) x5, sc 3, begin an inc with a sc, *grab Kermit's Right Arm and with the thumb facing forward, place it so the first st at the top lines

up with the last st of the round on the Body and sc them together in the same st to finish the inc* [30]

Rnd 20. Sc the next 2 st of the Arm and Body together, sc 12, *grab Kermit's Left Arm and place it so the 3 st at the top line up with the next 3 st on the Body and sc them together*, sc 13 [30 st and 2 Arms]

Rnds 21–22. Sc in each st around [2 rnds of 30 st]

Rnd 23. (Sc 4, inc) x6 [36]

Rnd 24. (Sc 5, inc) x6 [42]

Rnds 25–26. Sc in each st around [2 rnds of 42 st]

Rnd 27. (Sc 5, dec) x6 [36]

Rnd 28. (Sc 4, dec) x6 [30]

Finish stuffing the Head and begin stuffing the Body. Continue stuffing as you work the remaining rnds:

Rnd 29. (Sc 3, dec) x6 [24]

Rnd 30. (Sc 2, dec) x6 [18]

Rnd 31. (Sc, dec) x6 [12]

Rnd 32. (Dec) x6 [6]

Fasten off the yarn, leaving a short tail around 6 in. long. Use your needle to weave the tail through the front loops of the last rnd and pull tight to close. Pull the tail to the inside of the Body and trim any excess.

EYES (Make 2)

With White, make a magic ring

Rnd 1. Sc 6 in ring [6]

Rnd 2. (Inc) x6 [12]

Rnd 3. Sc in each st around [12]

Fasten off the yarn, leaving a short tail around 8-10 in. for attaching to the Head.

COLLAR

With Citron

Ch 4, (sl st in the second ch from the hook, sc, hdc, ch 5) x6, sl st in the second ch from the hook, sc, hdc [7 points]

Fasten off the yarn, leaving a tail around 16-18 in. long for attaching to the neck.

FEET (Make 2)

With Light Green, make a magic ring

Rnd 1. Sc 6 in ring [6]

Rnd 2. (Sc 2, inc) x2 [8]

Rnds 3–4. Sc in each st around [2 rnds of 8 st]

To make the toes we'll be making 4 picot st and crocheting the previous rnd closed: Each sc in the next rnd will be worked through 2 st from the previous rnd.

Rnd 5. (Picot: ch 3, sc in the back bump of the first ch made, sc previous rnd together) x3, picot: ch 3, sc in the back bump of the first ch made, sl st through the remaining 2 st from the previous rnd. [4 Picot toes, 3 sc, 1 sl st]

Fasten off the yarn and leave a short tail around 10-12 in. for attaching to the Leg. Use your needle to pull the tail through the inside of the foot and out through the heel to prepare for attaching to the Leg.

LEGS (Make 2)

With Light Green, make a magic ring

Rnd 1. Sc 8 in ring [8]

Rnds 2–19. Sc in each st around [18 rnds of 8 st]

Rnd 20. Press the previous rnd together so the st line up and sc them together [4]

Fasten off the yarn, leaving a short tail of around 8-10 in. for attaching to the Body.

ASSEMBLY

1. Embroider the pupils on the Eyes with a scrap of Black yarn and your needle. Make a small arc about 3 sc wide starting just above the bottom edge of the Eye. Make a vertical stitch over the center of the arc; make multiple passes to build up the pupil. Tie off your yarn on the inside of the Eye and trim the ends.

2. Add a small amount of stuffing to the Eyes and stitch them to the top of the Head about 2 st apart so that the pupils face front.

3. Wrap the Collar around the neck so that the ends meet and use the tail to stitch the inside edge of the Collar down so that the points are free to move.

4. Stitch the heels of the Feet to the bottom of the Legs (the ring and rnd 1). Be sure to stitch all the way around the Leg so that the Foot sits flat.

5. Stitch the Legs to the underside of the Body, slightly toward the front and about 2 st away from each other, with the Feet facing forward.

6. Cut a small heart shape out of pink felt for the tongue and use a hot glue gun to attach it inside of the Mouth.

Miss Piggy!

Miss Piggy is the ultimate diva, a fashion icon, a star of stage, screen, and all media known and unknown in perpetuity throughout the universe. She is invincible, indomitable, unstoppable, and yet very vulnerable—a side she only ever shows to her closest companions. After all, she's had to fight (sometimes literally) for everything she's achieved in life. And she intends to keep it all—the fame, the acclaim, and especially the jewelry. Miss Piggy adores the good things in life, especially chocolate.

FUN FACT Miss Piggy's over-the-top eye for fashion is legendary, and she's rarely seen without her signature pearls and gloves.

Miss Piggy

FINISHED MEASUREMENTS
Height: 8.5 in. / 21.5 cm
Width: 4.5 in. / 11.5 cm

YARN
Worsted weight (#4 medium) yarn, shown in Big Twist *Value* (100% acrylic, 380 yd. / 347 m per 6 oz. / 170 g skein)
Skin: Pale Peach
Hair: Pale Yellow
Dress/Shoes: Magenta
Gloves/Belt: Medium Rose
Eyelashes: Black
Eye Shadow: Lilac

HOOK
US F-5 / 3.75 mm hook

NOTIONS
• Polyester stuffing
• White, magenta, and blue Felt
• Pair of 6 mm plastic safety eyes
• Tapestry needle
• Removable stitch markers
• Hot glue gun
• Stretch Magic 0.5 mm clear bead and jewelry cord
• A string of mini pearl beads

GAUGE
Gauge is not critical for this project. Ensure your stitches are tight so the stuffing won't show through

---

SPECIAL STITCHES
Back Loop Only (BLO): Work through back loop only
Front Loop Only (FLO): Work through front loop only
Pop4: Popcorn st with 4 dc

NOTE
The Head/Body and the Arms are separate pieces that get crocheted together, so it is important to make them in order.

For more information on how to make Miss Piggy, including tips, step-by-step pictures, and videos, scan this QR code!

ARMS (Make 1 Right and 1 Left)

With Medium Rose, make a magic ring

Rnd 1. Sc 6 in ring [6]

Rnd 2. (Inc) x6 [12]

Rnd 3. *Right Arm:* Ch 3, starting in the second ch from the hook sc 2, in FLO sl st, (sl st, ch 4, starting in the second ch from the hook sc 3) x3, through both loops sc 7 [12 st and 4 fingers]

Left Arm: In FLO (sl st, ch 4, starting in the second ch from the hook sc 3) x3, sl st 2 on the ring, ch 3, starting in the second ch from the hook sc 2, through both loops sc 7 [12 st and 4 fingers]

Rnd 4. In BLO (using the back loops from rnd 2) sc 5, through both loops sc 7 [12]

Rnd 5. (Sc 4, dec) x2 [10]

Rnds 6–9. Sc in each st around, on the last st of rnd 9 change to Pale Peach [4 rnds of 10 st]

Rnd 10. In BLO sc in the back loops of each st around [10] Add stuffing to the hand; the rest of the Arm remains unstuffed

Rnds 11–13. Sc in each st around [3 rnds of 10 st]

Rnd 14. (Sc 3, dec) x2 [8]

Rnd 15. Sc 2, press the previous rnd together so the st line up and sc them together [4]

Fasten off the yarn, leaving a short tail of around 8-10 in. for attaching to the Body.

HEAD AND BODY

With Pale Peach, make a magic ring

Rnd 1. Sc 6 in ring [6]

Rnd 2. (Inc) x6 [12]

Rnd 3. (Sc, inc) x6 [18]

Rnd 4. (Sc 2, inc) x6 [24]

Rnd 5. (Sc 3, inc) x6 [30]

Rnds 6–8. Sc in each st around [3 rnds of 30 st]

Rnd 9. (Sc 4, inc) x6 [36]

Rnd 10. (Sc 5, inc) x6 [42]

Rnds 11–12. Sc in each st around [2 rnds of 42 st]

Insert safety eyes into blue felt and trim to make a small circle around each eye. Insert the eye with the blue felt into white felt and trim to make an almond shape around each eye. Insert the eyes with both layers of felt in between rnds 8 and 9, around 5 st apart. Tilt the felt so it is on a 45° angle, with the inside corner of the white felt around the eye on the higher side.

Rnd 13. (Sc 6, inc) x6 [48]

Rnds 14–16. Sc in each st around [3 rnds of 48 st]

Rnd 17. (Dec) x24 [24] Begin stuffing the Head fully and continue stuffing as you go. Be sure to get stuffing into the cheeks.

Rnd 18. (Sc 2, dec) x6 [18]

Rnd 19. (Sc, dec) x6 [12]

Rnd 20. (Sc, inc) x6 [18]

Rnd 21. (Sc 2, inc) x6 [24]

Rnd 22. Sc in each st around [24]

Rnd 23. *Grab one of the Arms and place it so the 4 st at the top line up with the next 4 st on the body and sc them together*, sc 8, *grab the other Arm and attach in the same manner as the first* sc 8 [24 st with 2 Arms]

Rnds 24–25. Sc in each st around [2 rnds of 24 st]

Rnd 26. (Sc 2, dec) x6 [18]

Rnd 27. Sc in each st around, on the last st of the rnd change to Magenta [18]

Rnd 28. (Sc 2, inc) x6 [24]

Rnd 29. Sc 3, inc) x6 [30]

Rnd 30. (Sc 4, inc) x6 [36]

Rnds 31–32. Sc in each st around [2 rnds of 36 st]

Rnd 33. (Sc 4, dec) x6 [30]

Rnd 34. (Sc 3, dec) x6 [24] Begin stuffing the Body fully and continue stuffing as you go:

Rnd 35. (Sc 2, dec) x6 [18]

Rnd 36. (Sc, dec) x6 [12]

Rnd 37. (Dec) x6 [6]

Fasten off the yarn, leaving a short tail around 6 in. long. Use your yarn needle to weave the tail through the front loops of the last rnd and pull tight to close. Pull the tail to the inside of the body and trim any excess.

PEARL NECKLACE

String a number of mini pearl beads on to a length of Stretch Magic bead and jewelry cord, until it fits snugly around Miss Piggy's neck. Tie off the cord, making several knots to keep the pearls in place. Leave the necklace on while you make and assemble the rest of Miss Piggy.

EARS (Make 2)

With Pale Peach, make a magic ring

Rnd 1. Sc 6 in ring [6]

Rnd 2. (Sc 2, inc) x2 [8]

Rnds 3–5. Sc in each st around [3 rnds of 8 st]

Rnd 6. Press the previous rnd together so the st line up and sc them together [4]

Fasten off the yarn, leaving a short tail around 8-10 in. for attaching to the Head.

SNOUT

With Pale Peach, make a magic ring

Rnd 1. Sc 6 in ring [6]

Rnd 2. (Sc 3 in the same st, inc, sc) x2 [12]

Rnd 3. Sc 2, inc, sc 5, inc, sc 3 [14]

Rnd 4. In BLO sc in the back loops of each st around [14]

Rnd 5. Sc in each st around [14]

Fasten off the yarn, leaving a short tail of around 8-10 in. for attaching to the face.

LOWER LIP

With Pale Peach

Ch 7, starting in the second chain from the hook hdc 6.

Fasten off the yarn, leaving a short tail of around 8-10 in. for attaching to the Head.

HAIR

With Pale Yellow, make a magic ring

Rnd 1. Sc 6 in ring [6]

Rnd 2. (Inc) x6 [12]

Rnd 3. (Sc, inc) x6 [18]

Rnd 4. (Sc 2, inc) x6 [24]

Rnd 5. (Ch 7, starting in the second ch from the hook sc 6, sl st in the next st on the circle) x5,

Rnd 5a. Ch 21, starting in the second ch from the hook (hdc inc) x10, sc 10, sl st in the next st on the circle

Rnd 5b. Ch 16, starting in the second ch from the hook (hdc inc) x10, sc 5, sl st in the next st on the circle.

Repeat rnds 5a and 5b all the way around the circle, ending on a 5a rnd [5 bangs strands, 10 long curly strands, 9 short curly strands]

Fasten off the yarn, leaving a long tail of around 22-24 in. for attaching to the Head.

LEGS (Make 2)

With Magenta, make a magic ring

Rnd 1. Sc 6 in ring [6]

Rnd 2. (Sc 3 in the same st, inc, sc) x2 [12]

Rnd 3. Sc, (inc) x3, sc 3, inc, pop4, inc, sc 2 [17]

Rnd 4. Sc 12, inc in the space of the pop4 from the previous rnd, sc 4 [18]

Rnd 5. Sc in each st around [18]

Rnd 6. (Dec) x4, sc 10, on the last st of the rnd change to Pale Peach [14]

Rnd 7. (Dec) x2, sc 10 [12]

Rnds 8–11. Sc in each st around [4 rnds of 12 st]

Add stuffing to the foot; the rest of the Leg remains unstuffed:

Rnd 12. (Sc 4, dec) x2 [10]

Rnd 13. Sc in each st around [10]

Rnd 14. (Sc 3, dec) x2 [8]

Rnd 15. Sc, press the top of the Leg together so the st line up and sc them together [3]

Fasten off the yarn, leaving a short tail of around 8-10 in. for attaching to the Body.

DRESS

The dress is made from the bottom up and in joining rnds. At the end of each rnd, sl st into the first st of the rnd and ch 1. The next rnd begins in the same space as the sl st.

Rnd 1. With Magenta ch 42, make sure the ch is not twisted and sl st into the first ch made and ch 1

Rnd 2. Sc in each ch around, sl st join and ch 1 [42]

Rnd 3. (Sc 5, dec) x6, sl st join and ch 1 [36]

Rnds 4–6. Sc in each st around, sl st join and ch 1 [3 rnds of 36 st]

Rnd 7. (Sc 4, dec) x6, sl st join and ch 1 [30]

Rnds 8–10. Sc in each st around, sl st join and ch 1 [3 rnds of 30 st]

Rnd 11. (Sc 3, dec) x6, on the last st of the rnd change to Medium Rose, sl st join and ch 1 [24]

Rnd 12. (Sc 2, dec) x6, sl st join and ch 1 [18]

Rnd 13. Sc in each st around, on the last st of the rnd change to Magenta, sl st join and ch 1 [18]

Rnd 14. (Sc 2, inc) x6, sl st join and ch 1 [24]

Rnds 15–16. Sc in each st around, sl st join and ch 1 [2 rnds of 24 st]

Rnd 17. Sc 3, ch 4, skip 4 st, sc 10, ch 4, skip 4 st, sc 3, sl st join and ch 1 [24 st with 2 armholes]

Rnd 18. Sc 8, skip 1 st, dc 4 in the same st, skip 1 st, sl st 2, skip 1 st, dc 4 in the same st, skip 1 st, sc 8 [26]

Fasten off the yarn and weave in the ends. Set aside for now.

ASSEMBLY

1. Add a little stuffing to the Snout and sew it to rnds 11–14 of the face with the longer side of the oval sitting horizontally.

2. Stitch one side of the Lower Lip in a half circle directly underneath the Snout so that the ends touch the underside of the Snout. Cut a piece of magenta felt to fit inside the Mouth and hot glue it in place.

3. Use Lilac and a needle to embroider the eye shadow on the upper portion of the white felt around the eyes. Make multiple passes to build up the color before tying off the yarn and weaving in the ends.

4. Use Black to embroider eyelashes that curve along the widest portion of the eye, that rests on the top of the safety eye, make 2 passes for thick luxurious lashes.

5. Attach the top of the Legs to the bottom of the Body so that they meet in the center; make sure the feet are facing forward.

6. Pull the Dress up from the bottom of the Body with the dc st facing forward. Pull the Arms through the armholes.

7. Place the Hair on top of the Head and angle it so that the bottom of the bangs reaches the top of the eyes, use the tail to stitch the circle portion of the Hair in place. Then space the long curly strands evenly around the sides and back of the Head and make a stitch near the middle of each strand to keep it in place. Repeat this with the short curly strands and try to cover up any bald spots between the long curly strands, underneath.

8. Stitch the Ears to the top of the head around 2 st away from the top center. Curve the bottom edge of the Ear slightly.

32

Fozzie Bear!

Fozzie Bear is the world's funniest—and only—stand-up comedy bear. From his beat-up hat to the trademark "Wocka-Wocka!" that punctuates his punchlines, Fozzie is comic through and through. His jokes aren't great ... okay, they aren't usually even good, but they are always delivered with passion, gusto, and the ever-dashed hope that this time they'll get a laugh. Fozzie is perseverance personified. Despite incessant heckling from Statler and Waldorf, he never gives up ... and never lets down The Muppets.

FUN FACT Fozzie has attributed some of his best jokes to a comedy writer named Gags Beasley, the author of the famous "Banana Sketch."

Fozzie Bear

FINISHED MEASUREMENTS

Height: 9 in. / 23 cm
Width: 4 in. / 10 cm

YARN

Worsted weight (#4 medium) yarn, shown in Big Twist *Value* (100% acrylic, 380 yd. / 347 m per 6 oz. / 170 g skein)
Body/Head: Mustard
Mouth: Varsity Red
Scarf: White
Hat/Eyebrows: Toffee
Hat: Black
Eyelids: Light Purple

Worsted weight (#4 medium) yarn shown in Red Heart *Super Saver* (100% acrylic, 364 yd. / 333 m per 7 oz. / 198 g skein)
Nose/Scarf: Light Raspberry

HOOK

US F-5 / 3.75 mm hook

NOTIONS

- Pink felt for the tongue
- White felt for the eyes
- Pair of 6 mm black plastic safety eyes
- Polyester stuffing
- Tapestry needle
- Hot glue gun
- Removable stitch markers

GAUGE

Gauge is not critical for this project. Ensure your stitches are tight so the stuffing won't show through.

SPECIAL STITCHES

Back Loop Only (BLO): Work through back loop only
Front Loop Only (FLO): Work through front loop only
Pop3: Popcorn stitch with 3 DC

NOTE

The Mouth, Head/Body, and Arms are separate pieces that get crocheted together, so it is important to make them in order.

For more information on how to make Fozzie Bear, including tips, step-by-step pictures, and videos, scan this QR code!

MOUTH

With Varsity Red, make a magic ring

Rnd 1. Sc 6 in ring [6]

Rnd 2. (Inc) x6 [12]

Rnd 3. (Sc, inc) x6 [18]

Rnd 4. (Sc 2, inc) x6 [24]

Rnd 5. (Sc 3, inc) x6 [30]

Fasten off the yarn and set aside for now.

ARMS (Make 2)

With Mustard, make a magic ring

Rnd 1. Sc 6 in ring [6]

Rnd 2. (Inc) x6 [12]

Rnd 3. (Sc 2, inc) x4 [16]

Rnd 4. Sc in each st around [16]

Rnd 5. Sc, pop3, sc 14 [16]

Rnd 6. (Sc 2, dec) x4 [12]

Rnd 7. Sc in each st around [12]

Rnd 8. (Sc 4, dec) x2 [10]

Rnds 9–16. Sc in each st around, after a few rnds add stuffing to the bottom of the Arms only, do not stuff the whole Arm [8 rnds of 10 st]

Rnd 17. (Sc 3, dec) x2 [8]

Rnd 18. Press the previous rnd together so the st line up and sc them together [4]

Fasten off the yarn and weave in the ends.

HEAD AND BODY

With Mustard, make a magic ring

Rnd 1. Sc 6 in ring [6]

Rnd 2. (Inc) x6 [12]

Rnd 3. (Sc, inc) x6 [18]

Rnds 4–7. Sc in each st around [4 rnds of 18 st]

Rnd 8. (Sc 2, inc) x6 [24]

Rnds 9–10. Sc in each st around [2 rnds of 24 st]

Rnd 11. (Sc 3, inc) x6 [30]

Rnd 12. (Sc 4, inc) x6 [36]

Rnds 13–14. Sc in each st around [2 rnds of 36 st]

Rnd 15. Sc, *grab the Mouth and line it up with the Head, right sides facing out, so the next Mustard st lines up with the last st that was made on the Mouth. Insert hook through both the Mustard and Varsity Red st and crochet them together* sc 15, *work the rest of the rnd in the Mustard st* sc 20 [36]

Insert safety eyes into white felt and trim to make a small oval around each eye. Insert the eyes with the felt in between rnds 10 and 11, around 2 st apart, centered above the Mouth.

Take a scrap of Light Purple and your needle to embroider some Eyelids on the top half of the white felt oval. Make several passes with the yarn and end with the yarn inside; weave in the ends.

Take a scrap of Toffee and your needle to embroider some Eyebrows about 2 st wide, around 2 rnds up from the tops of the eyes.

Rnd 16. Sc, *work into the Varsity Red on the bottom half of the mouth* sc 15, *work the rest of the rnd in the Mustard st* sc 20 [36]

Rnd 17. Sc, sc BLO 15, sc 20 [36]

Rnd 18. Sc in each st around [36]

Rnd 19. (Sc 4, dec) x6 [30]

Rnd 20. (Sc 3, dec) x6 [24]

Begin stuffing the Head—add just enough stuffing so that the Head keeps its shape without causing the Mouth to bulge.

Rnd 21. (Sc 2, dec) x6 [18]

Rnd 22. (Sc, dec) x6 [12]

Rnd 23. (Sc, inc) x6 [18]

Rnd 24. (Sc 2, inc) x6 [24]

Rnd 25. (Sc 3, inc) x6 [30]

Rnd 26. *Grab one of the Arms and place it so the 4 st at the top line up with the next 4 st on the body, and the thumb is facing forward, and sc them together*, sc 11, *grab the other Arm and attach in the same manner as the first* sc 11 [30 st with 2 arms]

Rnd 27. Sc in each st around [30]

Rnd 28. (Sc 4, inc) x6 [36]

Rnds 29–30. Sc in each st around [2 rnds of 36 st]

Rnd 31. (Sc 5, inc) x6 [42]

Rnds 32–36. Sc in each st around [5 rnds of 42 st]

Rnd 37. (Sc 5, dec) x6 [36]

Rnd 38. (Sc 4, dec) x6 [30]

Rnd 39. (Sc 3, dec) x6 [24]

Begin stuffing the Body and continue stuffing as you work the remaining rnds.

Rnd 40. (Sc 2, dec) x6 [18]

Rnd 41. (Sc, dec) x6 [12]

Rnd 42. (Dec) x6 [6]

Fasten off the yarn, leaving a short tail around 6 in. long. Use your needle to weave the tail through the front loops of the last rnd and pull tight to close. Pull the tail to the inside of the Body and trim any excess.

LEGS (Make 2)

With Mustard, make a magic ring

Rnd 1. Sc 6 in ring [6]

Rnd 2. (Sc 3 in the same st, inc, sc) x2 [12]

Rnd 3. Sc, (inc) x3, sc 3, (inc) x3, sc 2 [18]

Rnd 4. Sc 1, (sc, inc) x3, sc 3, (sc, inc) x3, sc 2 [24]

Rnd 5. Sc 2, (sc, inc) x3, sc 6, (sc, inc) x3, sc 4 [30]

Rnds 6–7. Sc in each st around [2 rnds of 30 st]

Rnd 8. Sc 2, (dec) x6, sc 16 [24]

Rnd 9. (Sc 2, dec) x6 [18]

Rnds 10–13. Sc in each st around [4 rnds of 18 st]

Rnd 14. (Sc 4, dec) x3 [15]

Add stuffing to the foot and partially up the Leg; do not stuff the full Leg.

Rnds 15–17. Sc in each st around [3 rnds of 15 st]

Rnd 18. (Sc 3, dec) x3 [12]

Rnds 19–20. Sc in each st around [2 rnds of 12 st]

Rnd 21. Sc, press the previous rnd together so the st line up and sc them together [6]

EARS (Make 2)

With Mustard, make a magic ring

Rnd 1. Sc 6 in ring [6]

Rnd 2. (Inc) x6 [12]

Rnd 3. (Sc 2, inc) x4 [16]

Rnd 4. Sc in each st around [16]

Rnd 5. (Sc 2, dec) x4 [12]

Rnd 6. (Dec) x6 [6]

Fasten off the yarn, leaving a tail around 8-10 in. long for closing the Ear and attaching it to the Head. Flatten the Ear and use your needle and the tail to stitch the last rnd of the Ear closed; do not trim the yarn yet.

NOSE

With Light Raspberry, make a magic ring

Rnd 1. Sc 8 in ring [8]

Rnd 2. Sc in each st around [8]

Fasten off the yarn, leaving a tail around 8-10 in. for attaching to the Head.

HAT

With Toffee, make a magic ring

Rnd 1. Sc 6 in ring [6]

Rnd 2. (Inc) x6 [12]

Rnd 3. (Sc, inc) x6 [18]

Rnd 4. In BLO sc in each st around [18]

Rnd 5. Sc in each st around, on the last st of the rnd change to Black yarn [18]

Rnd 6. Sc in each st around, on the last st of the rnd change to Toffee yarn [18]

Rnd 7. Sc in each st around [18]

Rnd 8. In FLO (sc 2, inc) x6 [24]

Rnd 9. (Sc 3, inc) x6 [30]

Fasten off the yarn, leaving a tail around 16-18 in. long for attaching to the Head. Use your needle to travel the tail to where the brim meets the side of the Hat—this is where it will be attached to the Head during assembly.

SCARF BASE

Row 1. Ch 41 in White, turn

Row 2. Sc 1 in the back bump of the second ch from the hook and change to

42

Light Raspberry, sc 1 in the back bump and change to White, repeat alternating between White and Light Raspberry through the end of the row (ending on Light Raspberry): Ch 1 in White and turn. [40]

Row 3. Sc in each st across in White [40]

Fasten off both yarns and weave in all of the ends.

SCARF BOW

Row 1. Ch 8 in White, turn

Row 2. Hdc in the second ch from the hook, hdc, sc 3, hdc 2, ch 1 and turn [7]

Row 3. Hdc and change to Light Raspberry, hdc and change to White, sc and change to Light Raspberry, sc and change to White, sc and change to Light Raspberry, hdc and change to White, hdc, ch 1 and turn [7]

Row 4. In White hdc 2, sc 3, hdc 2

Fasten off the yarns, leaving a White tail around 20-22 in. for attaching to the Scarf Base and Body. Weave in all ends except for the long tail.

ASSEMBLY

1. Stitch the Ears on either side of the Head around rnds 6-8.

2. Stitch the Hat to the top of the Head, along the inside of the brim. Fold the brim up and push the top of the Hat down to touch the top of the Head.

3. Add a small amount of stuffing (optional) and stitch the Nose between and slightly beneath the eyes.

4. Stitch the Legs to the underside of the Body with the feet facing forward.

5. With your needle, travel the tail of the Scarf Bow to the center bottom of the Bow. Wrap the Scarf Base around the neck and cross the ends about halfway between the neck and the ends of the Scarf. Place the Bow on the spot where the Scarf ends cross and use your needle to stitch it in place making a vertical stitch over the center of the Bow. Make multiple passes to build up a "knot" in the center of the Bow.

6. Cut a small heart shape out of pink felt for the tongue and use a hot glue gun to attach it inside of the Mouth.

Animal!

Animal is the drummer with The Electric Mayhem, and the absolute embodiment of a completely unleashed, totally out-of-control rock 'n' roll wild man. His passions in life are drums, food, and his friends! And he pursues them all with reckless abandon. He is closest to Sgt. Floyd Pepper, who he looks at as a mentor and companion after Floyd took him in when he was just a baby. Animal has a heart of gold and a child-like sweetness. He is mostly nonverbal, using short phrases like "Drums! Drums!" or "Louder! Louder!"

FUN FACT When Animal is holding his bunny, he is totally calm. No one knows why. But everyone is very grateful.

Animal

FINISHED MEASUREMENTS
Height: 10 in. / 25.5 cm
Width: 4.5 in. / 11.5 cm

YARN
Worsted weight (#4 medium) yarn shown in Red Heart *Super Saver* (100% acrylic, 364 yd. /333 m per 7 oz. /198 g skein)
Arms/Head/Body: Carrot

Worsted weight (#4 medium) yarn shown in Big Twist *Value* (100% acrylic, 380 yd. / 347 m per 6 oz. / 170 g skein)
Eyes/Tooth: White
Mouth/Eyebrow: Black
Eyelids: Bright Orange
Nose: Deep Red
Chains: Soft Gray
Jacket: Varsity Yellow
Hair/Jacket: Varsity Red
Pants: Toffee
Belt: Cream
Hair: Magenta

HOOKS
US F-5 / 3.75 mm hook
US P / 12 mm hook (optional)

NOTIONS
• Pair of 8 mm black plastic safety eyes
• Red felt for tongue
• Polyester stuffing
• Tapestry needle
• Hot glue gun
• Removable stitch markers

GAUGE
Gauge is not critical for this project. Ensure your stitches are tight so the stuffing won't show through.

SPECIAL STITCHES
Back Loop Only (BLO): Work through back loop only
Front Loop Only (FLO): Work through front loop only
Picot (picot): Ch 3, sc into the back bump of first ch made
Sc2tog: Single crochet 2 stitches together

NOTE
The Mouth, Head/Body, and Arms are separate pieces that get crocheted together, so it is important to make them in order.

For more information on how to make Animal, including tips, step-by-step pictures, and videos, scan this QR code!

MOUTH

With Black, make a magic ring

Rnd 1. Sc 6 in ring [6]

Rnd 2. (Inc) x6 [12]

Rnd 3. (Sc, inc) x6 [18]

Rnd 4. (Sc 2, inc) x6 [24]

Rnd 5. (Sc 3, inc) x6 [30]

Rnd 6. (Sc 4, inc) x6 [36]

Fasten off the yarn and weave in the ends.

ARMS (Make 1 Right and 1 Left)

With Carrot, make a magic ring

Rnd 1. Sc 6 in ring [6]

Rnd 2. *Right Arm*: In FLO sl st, ch 3, starting in the second ch from the hook sc 2, sl st 2, (ch 4, starting in the second ch from the hook sc 3, sl st) x3, sc through both loops [4 fingers]

Left Arm: In FLO sl st, (ch 4, starting in the second ch from the hook sc 3, sl st) x3, sl st, ch 3, starting in the second ch from the hook sc 2, sl st, sc through both loops [4 fingers]

Rnd 3. In BLO (using the back loops from rnd 2) sc 5, sc through both loops [6]

Rnds 4–15. Sc in each st around [12 rnds of 6 st]

Rnd 16. Sc, Press the previous rnd together so the st line up and sc them together [3]

Fasten off the yarn and weave in the ends.

HEAD AND BODY

With Carrot, make a magic ring

Rnd 1. Sc 6 in ring [6]

Rnd 2. (Inc) x6 [12]

Rnd 3. (Sc, inc) x6 [18]

Rnd 4. (Sc 2, inc) x6 [24]

Rnd 5. (Sc 3, inc) x6 [30]

Rnd 6. (Sc 4, inc) x6 [36]

Rnds 7–10. Sc in each st around [4 rnds of 36 st]

Rnd 11. *Grab the Mouth and line it up with the Head, right sides facing out: Insert hook through both the orange and black st and crochet them together* sc 16, *work the rest of the rnd in the orange st* sc 20 [36]

Rnd 12. *Work into the black st on the bottom half of the mouth* sc 20, *work the rest of the rnd in the orange st* sc 20 [40]

Rnd 13. In BLO sc 20, through both loops dec, sc 16, dec [38]

Rnd 14. Sc, (sc, dec) x3, (dec, sc) x3, sc, dec, sc 14, dec [30]

Rnd 15. Sc, (dec) x6, sc 12, dec, sc, dec [22]

Rnd 16. (Sc, dec) x4, sc 10 [18]

Rnd 17. Sc in each st around [18]

Begin stuffing the head, but do not stuff the lower lip:

Rnd 18. (Sc, dec) x6 [12]

Rnds 19–22. Sc in each st around [4 rnds of 12 st]

Rnd 23. (Inc) x6, sc 6 [18]

Rnd 24. Sc in each st around [18]

Rnd 25. (Sc 2, inc) x6 [24]

Rnd 26. *Grab Animal's Right Arm and place it so the 3 st at the top line up with the next 3 st on the Body and sc them together*, sc 9, *grab Animal's Left Arm and attach in the same manner as the first* sc 9 [24 st with 2 Arms]

Rnds 27–37. Sc in each st around [11 rnds of 24 st]

Begin stuffing the Head and Body and continue stuffing as you go

Rnd 38. (Sc 2, dec) x6 [18]

Rnd 39. (Sc, dec) x6 [12]

Rnd 40. (Dec) x6 [6]

Fasten off the yarn, leaving a short tail around 6 in. Use your needle to weave the tail through the front loops of the last rnd and pull tight to close. Pull the tail to the inside of the body and trim any excess.

EYES (Make 2)

With White, make a magic ring

Rnd 1. Sc 6 in ring [6]

Rnd 2. (Inc) x6 [12]

Rnd 3. (Sc 5, inc) x2 [14]

Rnds 4–5. Sc in each st around [2 rnds of 14 st]

Insert 8 mm plastic safety eye in between rnds 3 and 4.

Fasten off the yarn, leaving a short tail around 8-10 in. for attaching to the Head.

EYELIDS (Make 2)

With Bright Orange and Black

Row 1. In Bright Orange ch 2, sc 3 in the second ch from the hook, ch 1 and turn [3]

Row 2. (Inc) x3, ch 1 and turn [6]

Row 3. (Sc, inc) x3, ch 1 and turn [9]

Row 4. (Sc 2, inc) x3, on the last st of the row change to Black, ch 1 and turn [12]

Rows 5–6. Sc in each st across, ch 1 and turn [2 rows of 12 st]

Fasten off each color of yarn, leaving a short tail of around 8-10 in. of each color for attaching to the Head.

UNDER EYE BAGS (Make 2)

With Bright Orange

Ch 6, starting in the second ch from the hook (sc, inc) x2, sc [7]

Fasten off the yarn, leaving a short tail of around 8-10 in. for attaching to the Head.

NOSE

With Deep Red, make a magic ring

Rnd 1. Sc 6 in ring [6]

Rnd 2. (Inc) x6 [12]

Rnds 3–4. Sc in each st around [2 rnds of 12 st]

Rnd 5. (Sc, dec) x4 [8]

Fasten off the yarn, leaving a short tail of around 8-10 in. for attaching to the Head.

LOWER LIP

With Carrot

Ch 18, starting in the second ch from the hook hdc 17 [17]

Fasten off the yarn, leaving a tail of around 20 in. for attaching to the Mouth.

LONG TOOTH (Make 2)

With White

Ch 3, sc in the back bump of the third ch from the hook [1]

Fasten off the yarn, leaving a short tail of around 4 in. for attaching to the Mouth.

SHORT TOOTH (Make 5)

With White

Ch 2, sl st in the back bump of the second ch from the hook [1]

Fasten off the yarn, leaving a short tail of around 4 in. for attaching to the Mouth.

LEGS (Make 2)

With Carrot, make a magic ring

Rnd 1. Sc 6 in ring [6]

Rnd 2. (Sc 3 in the same st, inc, sc) x2 [12]

Rnd 3. Sc, (inc) x3, sc 3, (inc) x3, sc 2 [18]

Rnd 4. Sc in each st around [18]

Rnd 5. (Dec) x4, sc 10 [14]

Rnd 6. (Dec) x2, sc 10 [12]

Rnd 7. (Sc, dec) x4 [8]

Rnds 8–18. Sc in each st around [11 rnds of 8 st]

Rnd 19. Sc, press the top of the leg together so the st line up and sc them together [3]

Fasten off the yarn, leaving a short tail of around 8-10 in. for attaching to the Body.

JACKET

Row 1. In Varsity Yellow ch 25, starting in the back bump of the second ch from the hook sc 24 in the back bumps of the ch, ch 1 and turn [24]

Rows 2–5. Sc in each st across, ch 1 and turn [4 rows of 24 st]

Row 6. Sc 2, ch 5, skip 5 st, sc 10, ch 5, skip 5 st, sc 2, ch 1 and turn [24 st with 2 armholes]

Row 7. Sc in each st and ch across, on the last st of the row change to Varsity Red ch 1 and turn [24]

Row 8. (Sc2tog, sc 2) x3, (sc 2, sc2tog) x3 [18]

Row 9. *Side 1:* Do not turn, continue down the side sc 6, (sc 2, ch 1, sc 2) in the corner

Bottom: Continue around the bottom of the Jacket, sc 22, (sc 2, ch 1, sc2) in the last st on the bottom

Side 2: Continue around to the other side of the Jacket sc 6 [42]

Fasten off the yarn and weave in the ends.

SLEEVES (Make 2)

Row 1. Join Varsity Yellow to the corner of one of the armholes, sc 10 around the armhole [10]

Row 2. (Sc 4, inc) x2 [12]

Row 3. (Sc, inc) x6 [18]

Row 4. Sc in each st around, on the last st of the rnd change to Varsity Red [18]

Row 5. Sc in each st around [18]

Fasten off the yarn and weave in the end.

COLLAR WITH CHAIN

With Soft Gray

Ch 17, starting in the second ch from the hook hdc 16, *switch to a 12 mm hook, or simply adjust your tension so the next portion is extremely loose* ch 13, starting in the second ch from the hook sl st 12. [16 with a 12 ch chain]

Fasten off the yarn, leaving a short tail of around 8-10 in. for attaching to the Body.

WRIST CUFF (Make 2)

With Soft Gray

Ch 8, starting in the second ch from the hook hdc 7 [7]

Fasten off the yarn, leaving a short tail of around 8-10 in. for attaching to the wrist.

PANTS

With Toffee

The pants are made from the top down and in joining rnds. At the end of each rnd, sl st into the first st of the rnd and ch 1. The next rnd begins in the same space as the sl st.

Rnd 1. Ch 24, make sure the ch is not twisted and sl st into the first ch made and ch 1

Rnds 2–9. Sc in each st around, sl st join and ch 1 [8 rnds of 24 st]

RIGHT PANT LEG

Rnd 10. Sc 12, skip 12 st and sl st join to the first st of the rnd and ch 1 [12]

Rnds 11–16. Sc in each st around, sl st join and ch 1 [6 rnds of 12 st]

Rnd 17. (Picot, skip 1 st, sl st) x6 [6 picot]

Fasten off the yarn and weave in the ends.

LEFT PANT LEG

Rnd 18. Join yarn to the st to the left of the Right Pant Leg, ch 1, starting in the same st as the ch 1 sc 12, sl st join and ch 1 [12]

Rnds 19–26. Sc in each st around, sl st join and ch 1 [8 rnds of 12 st]

Rnd 27. (Picot, skip 1 st, sl st) x6 [6 picot]

Fasten off the yarn and weave in the ends.

BELT

With Cream

Ch 59, starting in the second ch from the hook sl st 58 [58]

Fasten off the yarn and weave in the ends.

ASSEMBLY

1. Stuff and attach the Nose to the Head directly above the center of the Mouth.

2. Stuff and attach the Eyes 2 rnds up from the Nose, about 2 st apart, with the plastic safety eyes facing front.

3. Starting with the Black yarn tail, attach the Eyelid to the Eye, about 2 rnds up from the safety eye, so the back of the Eyelid touches the Head, weave in the ends. Use the Bright Orange tail to stitch the back of the Eyelid to the Head, around the Eye, weave in the ends.

4. Attach the Under Eye Bags at the base of each Eye, following the curve of the Eye.

5. Attach the Lower Lip around the bottom of the Mouth so it covers the color change. Be sure to stitch both the bottom and top edges down; weave in the ends.

6. Attach one of the Short Teeth to the center of the lower jaw, just behind the lower lip. Attach the remaining four Short Teeth with two on either side of the first one.

7. Attach the Long Teeth, one on either side of the Short Teeth.

8. Cut two short strands of Varsity Yellow yarn around 6 in. long. Pull the Jacket on and lace a strand through either side of the Jacket about 2 rows up from the bottom and tie them together with a small bow. Repeat with the second strand of yarn about 2 rows up from the previous bow.

9. Wrap the hdc portion of the Collar around Animal's neck and use the tail to stitch it together; weave in the ends.

10. Wrap the Wrist Cuffs around each of Animal's wrists and use the tail to stitch them together; weave in the ends.

11. Pull the Pants on as high as you are able to, cut a strand of Toffee yarn around 20 in. long and attach the Pants at the waist.

12. Attach the middle of the Belt to the center of the back of the Pants. Pull the ends to the front and tie a knot or two, leaving the ends to dangle.

13. Cut a large number of Black strands of yarn around 4-5 in. long. Using a Lark's Head knot attach them to the Black portion of the Eyelids. Unwind the fibers of the yarn and trim to the desired length.

14. Cut a large number of Varsity Red strands and a handful of Magenta and Bright Orange strands around 4-5 in. long. Using a Lark's Head knot, attach the strands to Animal's Head. Be sure to attach them under his chin, and on his cheeks between his Eyes and his Mouth, on either side of his Nose. The bulk of the strands should be Varsity Red but include some Magenta and Bright Orange as well. Unwind the fibers of each strand and trim the yarn to the desired length (shorter on the cheeks and under the chin, longer on top and back of the Head).

15. Cut a small, rounded half circle out of red felt and hot glue it to the inside of Animal's mouth for his tongue.

Dr. Bunsen Honeydew and Beaker!

Together, Bunsen and Beaker are the founders, head researchers and, respectively, chief tester and lead guinea pig of Muppet Labs. They truly believe that they are on the verge of a great scientific discovery.

Dr. Bunsen Honeydew wants to achieve scientific breakthroughs that will change the world. Beaker, his beleaguered assistant, simply wants to make it through another day without too much suffering. Bunsen and Beaker are virtually inseparable and have a deep respect and affection for each other, even though Bunsen frequently demonstrates this by accidentally blowing up Beaker.

Dr. Bunsen Honeydew

FINISHED MEASUREMENTS
Height: 7 in. / 17.8 cm
Width: 4 in. / 10 cm

YARN
Worsted weight (#4 medium) yarn, shown in
Loops & Threads *Impeccable* (100% acrylic,
285 yd. / 260 m per 4.5 oz. / 127.5 g skein)
Head/Body: Citron

Worsted weight (#4 medium) yarn, shown in
Big Twist *Value* (100% acrylic, 380 yd. / 347 m
per 6 oz. / 170 g skein)
Shirt: Ivory
Pants/Vest: Medium Gray
Tie: Varsity Red
Shoes/Glasses/Smile: Black
Lab Coat: White

HOOK
US F-5 / 3.75 mm hook

NOTIONS
• Polyester stuffing
• Tapestry needle
• Removable stitch markers

GAUGE
Gauge is not critical for this project. Ensure
your stitches are tight so the stuffing won't
show through.

SPECIAL STITCHES
Picot (picot): Ch 3, sc into the back bump of first
ch made
Sc2tog: Single crochet 2 stitches together

NOTE
The Arms and the Head/Body are separate pieces
that get crocheted together, so it is important to
make them in order.

For more information on how to make Bunsen Honeydew, including tips,
step-by-step pictures, and videos, scan this QR code!

ARMS (MAKE 2)

With Citron make a Magic ring

Rnd 1. Sc 6 in ring [6]

Rnd 2. (Inc) x6 [12]

Rnds 3–4. Sc in each st around [2 rnds of 12 st]

Rnd 5. (Sc, dec) x4, on the last st of the rnd change to Ivory yarn [8]

Rnds 6–19. Sc in each st around [14 rnds of 8 st]

Add stuffing to the hand; the rest of the Arm remains unstuffed:

Rnd 20. Press the previous rnd together so the st line up and sc them together [4]

Fasten off the yarn and weave in the ends.

HEAD AND BODY

With Citron make a magic ring

Rnd 1. Sc 6 in ring [6]

Rnd 2. (Inc) x6 [12]

Rnd 3. (Sc, inc) x6 [18]

Rnd 4. (Sc 2, inc) x6 [24]

Rnd 5. (Sc 3, inc) x6 [30]

Rnds 6–8. Sc in each st around [3 rnds of 30 st]

Rnd 9. (Sc 4, inc) x6 [36]

Rnd 10. (Sc 5, inc) x6 [42]

Rnds 11–13. Sc in each st around [3 rnds of 42 st]

Rnd 14. (Sc 5, dec) x6 [36]

Rnd 15. (Sc 4, dec) x6 [30]

Begin stuffing the Head fully and continue stuffing as you go:

Rnd 16. (Sc 3, dec) x6 [24]

Rnd 17. (Sc 2, dec) x6 [18]

Rnd 18. (Sc, dec) x6, on the last st of the rnd change to Ivory yarn [12]

Rnd 19. (Sc, inc) x6 [18]

Rnd 20. (Sc 2, inc) x6 [24]

Rnd 21. *Grab one of the Arms and place it so the 4 st at the top line up with the next 4 st on the body and sc them together*, sc 8, *grab the other Arm and attach in the same manner as the first*, sc 8 [24 st with 2 Arms]

Rnds 22–28. Sc in each st around, on the last st of rnd 28 change to Medium Gray [7 rnds of 24 st]

Rnds 29–30. Sc in each st around [2 rnds of 24 st]

Begin stuffing the Body fully and continue stuffing as you go:

Rnd 31. (Sc 2, dec) x6 [18]

Rnd 32. (Sc, dec) x6 [12]

Rnd 33. (Dec) x6 [6]

Fasten off the yarn, leaving a short tail around 6 in. long. Use your needle to weave the tail through the front loops of the last rnd and pull tight to close. Pull the tail to the inside of the Body and trim any excess.

TIE

With Varsity Red

Ch 7, starting in the second ch from the hook sc 5, sl st [6]

Fasten off the yarn, leaving a short tail of around 8-10 in. for attaching to the Body.

VEST

With Medium Gray

The vest is made from the bottom up and in joining rnds. At the end of each rnd, sl st into the first st of the rnd and ch 1. The next rnd begins in the same space as the sl st.

Rnd 1. Ch 24, make sure the ch is not twisted and sl st into the first ch made and ch 1

Rnd 2. Sc in each ch around, sl st join and ch 1 [24]

Rnds 3–8. Sc in each st around, sl st join and ch 1 [6 rnds of 24 st]

Rnd 9. Sc 3, ch 4, skip 4 st, sc 10, ch 4, skip 4 st, sc 3, sl st join and ch 1 [24 st with 2 armholes]

Rnd 10. Sc 7, sl st 10, sc 7, sl st join [24]

Fasten off the yarn and weave in the tail. Set aside for now.

LEGS (Make 2)

With Black, make a magic ring

Rnd 1. Sc 6 in ring [6]

Rnd 2. (Sc 3 in the same st, inc, sc) x2 [12]

Rnd 3. Sc, (inc) x3, sc 3, (inc) x3, sc 2 [18]

Rnds 4–5. Sc in each st around [2 rnds of 18 st]

Rnd 6. (Dec) x4, sc 10 [14]

Rnd 7. (Dec) x2, sc 10, on the last st of the rnd change to Medium Gray yarn [12]

Rnds 8–11. Sc in each st around [4 rnds of 12 st]

Add stuffing to the foot; the rest of the Leg remains unstuffed:

Rnd 12. (Sc 4, dec) x2 [10]

Rnd 13. Sc in each st around [10]

Rnd 14. (Sc 3, dec) x2 [8]

Rnd 15. Sc, press the top of the Leg together so the st line up and sc them together [3]

Fasten off the yarn, leaving a short tail of around 8-10 in. for attaching to the Body.

LAB COAT

With White

Row 1. Ch 37, starting in the second ch from the hook sc 36, ch 1 and turn [36]

Rows 2–15. Sc in each st across, ch 1 and turn [14 rows of 36 st]

Row 16. Sc 5, ch 8, skip 8 st, sc 10, ch 8, skip 8 st, sc 5, ch 1 and turn [36 st with 2 armholes]

Row 17. Sc in each st and ch across, ch 1 and turn [36]

Row 18. (Sc2tog, sc 4) x3, (sc 4, sc2tog) x3, do not ch 1 [30]

Row 19. *Side 1:* Do not turn, picot and continue down the side, dc 3, hdc 2, sc 12, (sc 2, ch 1, sc 2) in the last st on the side

Bottom: Continue around the bottom of the Lab Coat sc 35, (sc 2, ch 1, sc 2) in the last st on the bottom

Side 2: Continue around to the other side of the Lab Coat sc 12, hdc 2, dc 3, picot, sl st in same space as the last dc, ch 1

Top: Continue around to the top of the Lab Coat, (sc2tog, sc 3) x3, (sc 3, sc2tog) x3, ch 1 and turn [101 st and 2 picot st border]

Row 20: (Sc2tog, sc 2) x3, (sc 2, sc2tog) x3 [18]

Fasten off the yarn and weave in the ends.

SLEEVES (MAKE 2)

Row 1. Join White yarn to the corner of one of the armholes, sc 16 around the armhole [16]

Rows 2–12. Sc in each st around [11 rnds of 16 st]

Fasten off the yarn and weave in the ends.

NOSE

With Citron, make a magic ring

Sc 6 in ring, picot, sl st into the first st of the rnd [6 and a picot]

Fasten off the yarn, leaving a short tail around 8-10 in. for attaching to the Head.

ASSEMBLY

1. Sew the Nose to rnds 7-12 of the face with the picot st toward the top of the Head.

2. Bunsen's left ear: join Citron to the side of the Head, between rnds 9 and 10, dc 3 in the same space 2 rnds up, sl st 1 rnd up. Fasten off the yarn and weave in the ends. Bunsen's right ear: join Citron yarn to the side of the Head, between rnds 6 and 7, dc 3 in the same space 2 rnds down, sl st 1 rnd down. Fasten off the yarn and weave in the ends.

3. Use Black yarn and needle to embroider the glasses on. Make two small circles, around 3 rnds tall by 3 st wide, connected by a short line at the bridge of the Nose. Make two arms from the outside of the circles to just above the Ears; weave in the ends.

4. Use Black yarn to embroider a straight line around 3 sc long, 1 rnd down from the bottom of the Nose.

5. Attach the Tie to the center front of the shirt; make a horizontal stitch 2 sc wide and repeat several times to build up the "knot" at the top of the Tie and weave in the ends.

6. Pull the Vest up from the bottom of the Body with the 10 sl st in the front. Pull the Arms through the armholes.

7. Attach the top of the Legs to the bottom of the Body so that they meet in the center; make sure the feet are facing forward.

8. Pull the Lab Coat on, fold the lapels away from the center front of the Body and close the front of the Coat so the left side overlaps the right side. Use a strand of White yarn to sew the front of the Coat closed, from the bottom up, stopping when around 3 rnds of the Vest are still visible underneath; weave in the ends.

Beaker

FINISHED MEASUREMENTS
Height: 9 in. / 22.9 cm
Width: 5 in. / 12.7 cm

YARN
Worsted weight (#4 medium) yarn shown in Big Twist *Value* (100% acrylic, 380 yd. / 347 m per 6 oz. / 170 g skein)
Head/Hands: Light Rose
Shirt: Sage
Pants: Olive Drab
Shoes: Toffee
Shoes: Ivory
Hair: Orange
Eyes: White
Tie: Varsity Green

Worsted weight (#4 medium) yarn shown in Big Twist *Heather* (100% acrylic, 380 yd. / 347 m per 6 oz. / 170 g skein)
Lab Coat: Sage Heather

Worsted weight (#4 medium) yarn shown in Caron One Pound (100% acrylic, 812yd. / 742 m per 16 oz. / 454 g skein)
Nose: Living Coral

HOOK
US F-5 / 3.75mm hook

NOTIONS
- Pair of 6 mm black plastic safety eyes
- Red felt for mouth
- Polyester stuffing
- Tapestry needle
- Pet brush/comb
- Hot glue gun
- Removable stitch markers

GAUGE
Gauge is not critical for this project. Ensure your stitches are tight so the stuffing won't show through.

SPECIAL STITCHES
Picot (picot): Ch 3, sc into the back bump of first ch made
Sc2tog: Single crochet 2 stitches together

NOTE
The Arms and the Head/Body are separate pieces that get crocheted together, so it is important to make them in order.

For more information on how to make Beaker, including tips, step-by-step pictures, and videos, scan this QR code!

ARMS (Make 2)

With Light Rose, make a magic ring

Rnd 1. Sc 6 in ring [6]

Rnd 2. (Inc) x6 [12]

Rnds 3–4. Sc in each st around [2 rnds of 12 st]

Rnd 5. (Sc, dec) x4, on the last st of the rnd change to Sage yarn [8]

Rnds 6–21. Sc in each st around [16 rnds of 8 st]

Add stuffing to the hand; the rest of the Arm remains unstuffed.

Rnd 22. Press the previous rnd together so the st line up and sc them together [4]

Fasten off the yarn and weave in the ends.

HEAD AND BODY

With Light Rose, make a magic ring

Rnd 1. Sc 6 in ring [6]

Rnd 2. (Inc) x6 [12]

Rnd 3. (Sc, inc) x6 [18]

Rnds 4–18. Sc in each st around, on the last st of rnd 18 change to Sage yarn [15 rnds of 18 st]

Rnd 19. (Sc 2, inc) x6 [24]

Rnds 20–21. Sc in each st around [2 rnds of 24 st]

Rnd 22. *Grab one of the Arms and place it so the 4 st at the top line up with the next 4 st on the Body and sc them together*, sc 8, *grab the other Arm and attach in the same manner as the first*, sc 8 [24 st with 2 Arms]

Rnds 23–31. Sc in each st around, on the last st of rnd 31 change to Olive Drab yarn [9 rnds of 24 st]

Rnds 32–33. Sc in each st around [2 rnds of 24 st]

Begin stuffing the Head and Body fully, continue stuffing as you go:

Rnd 34. (Sc 2, dec) x6 [18]

Rnd 35. (Sc, dec) x6 [12]

Rnd 36. (Dec) x6 [6]

Fasten off the yarn, leaving a short tail around 6 in. Use your yarn needle to weave the tail through the front loops of the last rnd and pull tight to close. Pull the tail to the inside of the Body and trim any excess.

EYES (Make 2)

With White make a magic ring

Rnd 1. Sc 6 in ring [6]

Rnd 2. (Sc, inc) x3 [9]

Rnd 3. Sc in each st around [9]

Insert 6 mm safety eye through the center of the magic ring

Rnd 4. (Sc, dec) x3 [6]

Fasten off the yarn, leaving a short tail around 8-10 in. The back of the safety eye should help the Eye keep its shape, but if you'd like to add a small amount of stuffing, feel free to do so. Use your yarn needle to weave the tail through the front loops of the last rnd and pull tight to close. Do not trim the yarn.

NOSE

With Living Coral make a magic ring

Rnd 1. Sc 6 in ring [6]

Rnd 2. (Sc, inc) x3 [9]

Rnds 3–4. Sc in each st around [2 rnds of 9 st]

Rnd 5. (Sc, dec) x3 [6]

Add a small amount of stuffing.

Rnd 6. Press the previous rnd together so the st line up and sc them together [3]

Fasten off the yarn, leaving a short tail of around 8-10 in. for attaching to the Head.

HAIR CAP

With Orange make a magic ring

Rnd 1. Sc 6 in ring [6]

Rnd 2. (Inc) x6 [12]

Rnd 3. (Sc, inc) x6 [18]

Rnd 4. Sc in each st around [18]

Fasten off the yarn, leaving a medium length tail around 12-14 in. for attaching to the Head.

MOUTH

With Light Rose

Row 1. Ch 4, starting in the second ch from the hook sc 2, sc 3 in the same st, continue around to work on the other side of the ch, skip the first ch and sc 2, ch 1 and turn: [7]

Row 2. Sc 2, (inc) x3, sc 2 [10]

Fasten off the yarn, leaving a short tail of around 8-10 in. for attaching to the Head.

TIE

With Varsity Green

Ch 9, starting in the second ch from the hook sc 7, sl st [8]

Fasten off the yarn, leaving a tail around 8-10 in. for attaching to the Body.

SHIRT COLLAR

With Sage

Ch 19, in the second ch from the hook (dc, ch 1, dc), hdc, sc 14, hdc, (dc, ch 1, dc, sl st) in the last ch. [20]

Fasten off the yarn, leaving a medium length tail around 12–14 in. for attaching to the Body.

LEGS (Make 2)

With Toffee, make a magic ring

Rnd 1. Sc 6 in ring [6]

Rnd 2. (Sc 3 in the same st, inc, sc) x2 [12]

Rnd 3. Sc, (inc) x3, sc 3, (inc) x3, sc 2, on the last st of the rnd change to Ivory yarn [18]

Rnds 4–5. Sc in each st around [2 rnds of 18 st]

Rnd 6. (Dec) x4, sc 10 [14]

Rnd 7. (Dec) x2, sc 10, on the last st of the rnd change to Toffee yarn [12]

Rnd 8. Sc in each st around, on the last st of the rnd change to Olive Drab yarn [12]

Rnds 9–13. Sc in each st around [5 rnds of 12 st]

Add stuffing to the foot; the rest of the Leg remains unstuffed.

Rnd 14. (Sc 4, dec) x2 [10]

Rnd 15. Sc in each st around [10]

Rnd 16. (Sc 3, dec) x2 [8]

Rnd 17. Sc, press the top of the Leg together so the st line up and sc them together [3]

Fasten off the yarn, leaving a short tail of around 8-10 in. for attaching to the Body.

LAB COAT

With Sage Heather

Row 1. Ch 37, starting in the second ch from the hook sc 36, ch 1 and turn [36]

Rows 2–17. Sc in each st across, ch 1 and turn [16 rows of 36 st]

Row 18. Sc 5, ch 8, skip 8 st, sc 10, ch 8, skip 8 st, sc 5, ch 1 and turn [36 st with 2 armholes]

Row 19. Sc in each st and ch across, ch 1 and turn [36]

Row 20. (Sc2tog, sc 4) x3, (sc 4, sc2tog) x3, do not ch 1 [30]

Row 21. *Side 1:* Do not turn, picot and continue down the side, dc 3, hdc 2, sc 13, (sc 2, ch 1, sc 2) in the last st on the side

Bottom: Continue around the bottom of the Lab Coat sc 35, (sc 2, ch 1, sc 2) in the last st on the bottom

Side 2: Continue around to the other side of the Lab Coat sc 13, hdc 2, dc 3, picot, sl st in same space as the last dc, ch 1

Top: Continue around to the top of the Lab Coat, (sc2tog, sc 3) x3, (sc 3, sc2tog) x3, ch 1 and turn [101 st and 2 picot st border]

Fasten off the yarn and weave in the end.

SLEEVES (MAKE 2)

Row 1. Join Sage Heather yarn to the corner of one of the armholes, sc 16 around the armhole [16]

Rows 2–14. Sc in each st around [13 rnds of 16 st]

Fasten off the yarn and weave in the ends.

ASSEMBLY

1. Stitch the Hair Cap to the top of the Head.

2. Cut a piece of red felt in the same shape as the Mouth. Stitch the bottom edge of the Mouth one rnd up from the color change at the neck. Place the piece of red felt on the Head and trim the edges so that when the Mouth is folded up it covers the felt; hot glue the felt in place.

3. Stitch the top edge of the Nose around four rnds up from the top of the Mouth so that when the Nose is at a 45° angle it touches the top of the Mouth. Stitch about 2 rnds down from the top of the Nose on either side to secure the Nose in place.

4. Stitch the Eyes right next to each other, directly above the Nose. When attaching the second Eye, stitch the Eyes together at the center.

5. Attach the Tie to the center front of the shirt; make a horizontal stitch two sc wide and repeat several times to build up the "knot" at the top of the Tie and weave in the ends.

6. Place the Collar around the neck, covering the color change, and stitch the top edge down; weave in the ends.

7. Attach the top of the Legs to the bottom of the Body so that they meet in the center; make sure the feet are facing forward.

8. Pull the Lab Coat on, fold the lapels away from the center front of the Body and close the front of the Coat so the left side overlaps the right side. Use a strand of Sage Heather to sew the front of the Coat closed, from the bottom up, stopping when a few st of the Tie are still visible underneath; weave in the ends.

9. Use a strand of Toffee around 24 in. long to embroider the top part of the Shoes. Insert your needle toward the back of the foot below the color change and out the other side and pull the yarn so it is flat on the top of the foot. (Don't pull so tight that it makes the foot pucker.) Repeat about four times to build up the detail on the top of the foot.

10. Cut a large number of strands of Orange yarn around 4 in. long. Using a Lark's Head knot, attach the strands to the Hair Cap. (When attaching the strands be sure that your hook is always pointed to the top of the Head when first inserted; this will ensure that the knot is hidden) Attach the strands to each st of the outside rnd of the Hair Cap, and to around every other st on the top. Once the Hair Cap is covered, use a pet brush or comb to brush out the yarn strands until they resemble hair. Trim the hair to the desired length (around .5 in.–.75 in.) Gently twist each individual section of hair, to separate it into spikes.

FUN FACT Some of the most notable inventions to come out of Muppet Labs are edible paperclips, fireproof paper, and the gorilla detector.

The Great Gonzo and Camilla!

Dreaming of a life in show business from the time she was an egg, Camilla flew the coop, met Gonzo, and hatched a career as the biggest and most plucky performer of her generation. She acts, she dances, she clucks—she's a triple threat. Gonzo is a multitalented artiste, who sees every endeavor—from performance art, daredevil stunts, or plumbing—as an opportunity to create a masterpiece ... and break something. Whether he is balancing a piano on his nose or dancing barefoot in unpasteurized cottage cheese, Gonzo is committed to his art ... and fearless about the consequences.

The Great Gonzo

FINISHED MEASUREMENTS

Height: 8 in. / 20 cm
Width: 4 in. / 10 cm

YARN

Worsted weight (#4 medium) yarn, shown in Big Twist *Value* (100% acrylic, 380 yd. / 347 m per 6 oz. / 170 g skein)
Skin: Varsity Blue
Nose: Eggplant
Mouth: Varsity Red
Eyes/Shirt: White
Eyelid: Varsity Gold
Eyeliner: Evergreen
Suit: Purple
Suit Accents/Bow Tie: Plum
Shoes: Black

HOOK

US F-5 / 3.75 mm hook

NOTIONS

- Pair of 8 mm plastic safety eyes
- Polyester stuffing
- Yarn needle
- Removable stitch markers

GAUGE

Gauge is not critical for this project. Ensure your stitches are tight so the stuffing won't show through

SPECIAL STITCHES

Back Loop Only (BLO): Work through back loop only
Front Loop Only (FLO): Work through front loop only
Picot (picot): Ch 3, sc into the back bump of first ch made
Sc2tog: Single crochet 2 stitches together

NOTES

The Mouth, Nose, Head/Body, and Arms are separate pieces that get
crocheted together, so it is important
to make them in order.

For more information on how to make Gonzo, including tips, step-by-step pictures, and videos, scan this QR code!

MOUTH

With Varsity Red, make a magic ring

Rnd 1. Sc 6 in ring [6]

Rnd 2. (Inc) x6 [12]

Rnd 3. (Sc, inc) x6 [18]

Rnd 4. (Sc 2, inc) x6 [24]

Fasten off the yarn and weave in the ends.

NOSE

With Eggplant, make a magic ring

Rnd 1. Sc 6 in ring [6]

Rnd 2. (Inc) x6 [12]

Rnd 3. Sc in each st around [12]

Rnd 4. In BLO sl st 6, through both loops hdc 6 [12]

Rnd 5. In FLO from two rnds previous sc 6, through both loops sc 6 [12]

Rnds 6–13. Repeat rnds 4-5 four more times

Rnd 14. (Sc, inc) x6 [18]

Stuff the Nose loosely so it is still able to curl.

Rnd 15. Sc 3, *grab the Mouth and line it up with the Nose, wrong sides together. Insert hook through both the Eggplant st and the Varsity Red st* sc 7 *work the rest of the rnd in only the Eggplant st* sc 8 [18]

Rnd 16. Sc 3, *work into the Varsity Red st on the bottom half of the Mouth* sc 17 *work the rest of the rnd in only the Eggplant st* sc 8 [28]

Rnds 17–18. Sc in each st around [2 rnds of 28 st]

Rnd 19. Sc 6 *place stitch marker in the last st made*, sc 20, sc 3 in the same st, sc [30]

Fasten off the yarn and weave in the ends. Fold the Varsity Red Mouth portion in half, which should cause the lower section of the Eggplant yarn to fold in on itself to from the lower "lip."

ARMS (Make 2)

With Varsity Blue, make a magic ring

Rnd 1. Sc 6 in ring [6]

Rnd 2. In FLO (sl st in front loop, ch 4, starting in the second ch from the hook hdc 3) x3, sc 3 through both loops [3 fingers and 3 st]

Rnd 3. In BLO (using the back loops from rnd 2) sc 3, sc 3 through both loops, on the last st of the rnd change to White yarn [6]

Rnds 4–15. Sc in each st around [12 rnds of 6 st]

Rnd 16. Press the previous rnd together so the st line up and sc them together [3]

Fasten off the yarn and weave in the ends.

HEAD AND BODY

With Varsity Blue, make a magic ring

Rnd 1. Sc 6 in ring [6]

Rnd 2. (Inc) x6 [12]

Rnd 3. (Sc, inc) x6 [18]

Rnd 4. (Sc 2, inc) x6 [24]

Rnd 5. (Sc 3, inc) x6 [30]

Rnds 6–8. Sc in each st around [3 rnds of 30 st]

Rnd 9. (Sc 4, inc) x6 [36]

Rnd 10. (Sc 5, inc) x6 [42]

Rnd 11. *Grab the Nose/Mouth piece and line it up with the Head, right sides together, so the next st on the Head is lined up with the marked st from rnd 18 of the Nose/Mouth piece. Insert hook through both the Eggplant st and the Varsity Blue st* sc 17, *work the rest of the rnd in only the Varsity Blue st* sc 25 [42]

Rnd 12. *Work into the Eggplant st on the bottom half of the Nose/Mouth* sc 13, *work the rest of the rnd in only the Varsity Blue st* dec, sc 21, dec [36]

Rnd 13. Sc in each st around [36]

Rnd 14. (Sc 4, dec) x6 [30]

Begin stuffing the Head—add just enough stuffing so that the Head keeps its shape without causing the Mouth to bulge. Do not stuff the lower lip.

Rnd 15. (Sc 3, dec) x6 [24]

Rnds 16–17. Sc in each st around, on the last st of rnd 17 change to White yarn [2 rnds of 24 st]

Rnd 18. (Sc 3, inc) x6 [30]

Rnd 19. Sc 28, *Grab one of the Arms and place it so the 3 st at the top line up with the next 3 st on the body and sc the first 2 st of the Arm and the Body together* [30 with 1 Arm partially attached]

Rnd 20. *sc the third st of the Arm and body together*, sc 12, *grab the other Arm and place it so the next 3 st at the top line up with the next 3 st on the body and sc them together*, sc 14 [30 with 2 Arms]

Rnds 21–29. Sc in each st around, on the last st of rnd 29 change to Purple yarn [9 rnds of 30 st]

Rnds 30–32. Sc in each st around [3 rnds of 30 st]

Begin stuffing the Body fully and continue stuffing as you go:

Rnd 33. (Sc 3, dec) x6 [24]

Rnd 34. (Sc 2, dec) x6 [18]

Rnd 35. (Sc, dec) x6 [12]

Rnd 36. (Dec) x6 [6]

Fasten off the yarn, leaving a short tail around 6 in. Use your needle to weave the tail through the front loops of the last rnd and pull tight to close. Pull the tail to the inside of the Body and trim any excess.

EYES (Make 2)

With White, make a magic ring

Rnd 1. Sc 6 in ring [6]

Rnd 2. (Inc) x6 [12]

Rnd 3. Sc in each st around [12]

Fasten off the yarn, leaving a short tail of around 8-10 in. for attaching to the Head. Insert safety eye between rnds 2 and 3. The washer on the safety eye should eliminate the need for stuffing, but if you'd like to add a little, feel free to do so.

EYELIDS (Make 2)

Row 1. In Varsity Gold ch 2, starting in the second ch from the hook sc 3 in the same ch, ch 1 and turn [3]

Row 2. (Inc) x3, ch 1 and turn [6]

Row 3. (Sc, inc) x3, on the last st of the row change to Evergreen, ch 1 and turn [9]

Row 4. Sc in each st across [9]

Fasten off the yarns, leaving two short tails of around 8-10 in., one of each color for attaching to the Head. Weave in the shorter tails.

BOW TIE

With Plum

Ch 7, dc in the third ch from the hook, sc, sl st, sc, dc 2 in the same st.

Fasten off the yarn, leaving a medium length tail around 12-14 in. for attaching to the Body.

LEGS (Make 2)

With Black, make a magic ring

Rnd 1. Sc 6 in ring [6]

Rnd 2. (Sc 3 in the same st, inc, sc) x2 [12]

Rnd 3. Sc, (inc) x3, sc 3, (inc) x3, sc 2 [18]

Rnds 4–5. Sc in each st around [2 rnds of 18 st]

Rnd 6. (Dec) x4, sc 10 [14]

Rnd 7. (Dec) x2, sc 10, on the last st of the rnd change to Purple yarn [12]

Rnds 8–13. Sc in each st around [6 rnds of 12 st]

Add stuffing to the foot; the rest of the Leg remains unstuffed.

Rnd 14. (Sc 4, dec) x2 [10]

Rnd 15. Sc in each st around [10]

Rnd 16. (Sc 3, dec) x2 [8]

Rnd 17. Sc, press the top of the Leg together so the st line up and sc them together [3]

Fasten off the yarn, leaving a short tail of around 8-10 in. for attaching to the Body.

TUXEDO JACKET

With Purple

Row 1. Ch 31, starting in the back bump of the second ch from the hook sc 30 in the back bumps of the ch, ch 1 and turn [30]

Rows 2-7. Sc in each st across, ch 1 and turn [8 rows of 30 st]

Row 8. Sc2tog, sc 26, sc2tog, ch 1 and turn [28]

Row 9. Sc in each st across, ch 1 and turn [28]

Row 10. Sc2tog, sc 24, sc2tog, ch 1 and turn [26]

Row 11. Sc in each st across, ch 1 and turn [26]

Row 12. Sc 3, ch 5, skip 5 st, sc 10, ch 5, skip 5 st, sc 3, ch 1 and turn [26 st with 2 armholes]

Row 13. Sc in each st across, on the last st change to Plum yarn [26]

Row 14. *Side 1*: Do not turn, continue down the side, picot, dc 4, hdc 3, on the previous st change to Purple yarn, hdc 6, (hdc 2, ch 1, hdc 2) in the last st on the side

Bottom: Continue around the bottom of the jacket, skip 1 st, hdc 29, (hdc 2, ch 1, hdc2) in the last st on the bottom

Side 2: Continue around to the other side of the jacket, skip 1 st, hdc 6, on the previous st change to Plum yarn, hdc 3, dc 4, picot, sl st

Top: Continue around to the top of the jacket, (sc2tog) x2, ch 2, in BLO hdc 18, through both loops (sc2tog) x2 [85 st and 2 picot st]

Fasten off the yarn and weave in the ends.

SLEEVES (Make 2)

Rnd 1. Join Purple yarn to the corner of one of the armholes, sc 10 around the armhole [10]

Rnds 2–13. Sc in each st around [12 rnds of 10 st]

Fasten off the yarn and weave in the end.

ASSEMBLY

1. Stitch the Eyes directly behind the color change between the Nose and the Head, about one st apart. The safety eyes should be turned toward the center of the Head.

2. Use the Varsity Gold tail of the Eyelids to stitch the base of the Eyelid behind and around the Eyes. Use the Evergreen tail to stitch the eyeliner line across the tops of the Eyes.

3. Cut a strand of Varsity Blue yarn around 4 in. long. Use a Lark's Head knot to attach it to the very top of the Head, unwind the fibers of the yarn and trim to the desired length.

4. Grab the Bow Tie and weave in the shorter tail, weave the longer tail to the center of the Bow Tie. Make a vertical stitch 2 rnds tall at the top center of the shirt, catching the middle of the Tie. Make multiple passes in the same direction to build up the "knot" of the Bow Tie.

5. Attach the top of the Legs to the bottom of the Body so that they meet in the center; make sure the feet are facing forward.

6. Pull the Tuxedo Jacket on, fold the Plum lapels away from the center front of the Body and close the front of the Jacket so the left side overlaps the right side. Use a strand of Plum yarn to sew the Purple portion of the front closed, from the bottom up, forming two Plum "buttons," and embroider 2 horizontal lines about 3 st wide, 4 rows up from the bottom; weave in the ends. (Optional: Use Plum yarn to tack the lapels and collar down on the Jacket.)

Camilla the Chicken

FINISHED MEASUREMENTS
Height: 6 in. / 15.25 cm
Width: 3.5 in. / 9 cm

YARN
Worsted weight (#4 medium) yarn, shown in
Big Twist *Value* (100% acrylic, 380 yd. / 347 m
per 6 oz. / 170 g skein)
Feathers: White
Comb/Wattle: Deep Red
Eyelids: Varsity Blue
Eyeliner: Black

Worsted weight (#4 medium) yarn shown in Red
Heart *Super Saver* (100% acrylic, 364 yd. / 333 m
per 7 oz. / 198 g skein)
Beak: Carrot

HOOK
US F-5 / 3.75 mm hook

NOTIONS
• Pair of 6 mm black plastic safety eyes
• White felt
• Polyester stuffing
• Tapestry needle
• Removable stitch markers

GAUGE
Gauge is not critical for this project. Ensure
your stitches are tight so the stuffing won't
show through.

SPECIAL STITCHES
Back Loop Only (BLO): Work through back
loop only
Front Loop Only (FLO): Work through front
loop only
Picot (picot): Ch 3, sc into the back bump of first
ch made

For more information on how to make Camilla, including tips, step-by-
step pictures, and videos, scan this QR code!

HEAD AND BODY

With White, make a magic ring

Rnd 1. Sc 6 in ring [6]

Rnd 2. (Inc) x6 [12]

Rnd 3. (Sc, inc) x6 [18]

Rnd 4. (Sc 2, inc) x6 [24]

Rnd 5. (Sc 3, inc) x6 [30]

Rnds 6–13. Sc in each st around [8 rnds of 30 st]

Insert safety eyes into white felt and trim to make a small circle around each eye. Insert the eye with the felt in between rnds 7 and 8, about 4 st apart.

Take a scrap of Varsity Blue yarn and your needle to embroider some Eyelids on the top half of the white felt oval. Make several passes with the yarn and end with the yarn inside; weave in the ends.

Take a scrap of Black yarn and embroider on an Eyelash line between the Eyelids and the plastic safety eye and add a short perpendicular line to the outside edges of the Eyelashes.

Rnd 14. (Inc) x6, (sc 3, inc) x6 [42]

Rnd 15. (Sc, inc) x6, (sc 4, inc) x6 [54]

Rnds 16–19. Sc in each st around [4 rnds of 54 st]

Rnd 20. Sc 9, ch 6, starting in the back bump of the second ch from the hook sc 5, sc in the same space as the st at the base of the ch, sc 45 [65]

Rnd 21. Sc 13, sc 3 in the same st, continue around the other side of the ch, skip 1 st, sc 51 [66]

Rnds 22–25. Sc in each st around [4 rnds of 66 st]

Rnd 26. Sc 30, (sc 4, dec) x6 [60]

Rnd 27. (Sc 8, dec) x6 [54]

Rnd 28. (Sc 7, dec) x6 [48]

Rnd 29. (Sc 6, dec) x6 [42]

Rnd 30. (Sc 5, dec) x6 [36]

Begin stuffing the Head and Body fully, continue stuffing as you go.

Rnd 31. (Sc 4, dec) x6 [30]

Rnd 32. (Sc 3, dec) x6 [24]

Rnd 33. (Sc 2, dec) x6 [18]

Rnd 34. (Sc, dec) x6 [12]

Rnd 35. (Dec) x6 [6]

Fasten off the yarn, leaving a short tail around 6 in. Use your needle to weave the tail through the front loops of the last rnd and pull tight to close. Pull the tail to the inside of the Body and trim any excess.

COMB

With Deep Red

Row 1. Join yarn to the space in between rnds 6 and 7, sc 8 in a straight line up the front of the Head, working in between the rnds of the Head, ch 1 and turn [8]

Row 2. Picot, skip 1 st, sl st, skip 1 st, dc 4 in the same st, skip 1 st, sl st, picot, skip 1 st, sl st

Fasten off the yarn and weave in the ends.

BEAK

With Carrot, make a magic ring

Rnd 1. Sc 6 in ring [6]

Rnd 2. Sc 2, (inc) x2, sc 2 [8]

Rnd 3. Sc 3, (inc) x2, sc 3 [10]

Rnd 4. Sc in each st around [10]

Rnd 5. Press the previous rnd together so the st line up and sc through both front and back st, sc 2, inc, sc 2 [6]

Fasten off the yarn, leaving a short tail of around 8-10 in. for attaching to the Head.

WATTLE

With Deep Red

Ch 17, starting in the third ch from the hook dc, hdc, sl st 11, hdc, dc-sl in the same ch [15]

Fasten off the yarn, leaving a short tail of around 8-10 in. for attaching to the Head.

WINGS (Make 2)

With White, make a magic ring

Rnd 1. Sc 6 in ring [6]

Rnd 2. Sc 2, (inc) x2, sc 2 [8]

Rnd 3. Sc 3, (inc) x2, sc 3 [10]

Rnd 4. Sc 4, (inc) x2, sc 4 [12]

Rnd 5. (Sc 2, inc) x4 [16]

Rnds 6–7. Sc in each st around [2 rnds of 16 st]

Rnd 8. (Sc 2, dec) x4 [12]

Rnd 9. Press the previous rnd together so the st line up and sc them together [6]

Fasten off the yarn, leaving a short tail of around 8-10 in. for attaching to the Body.

LEGS (Make 2)

With Carrot, make a magic ring

Rnd 1. Sc 6 in ring [6]

Rnd 2. In FLO sl st, ch 3, starting in the second ch from the hook sc 2, sl st 2, (ch 3, starting in the second ch from the hook sc 2, sl st) x3 [3 talons on the front of the foot, 1 talon on the back]

Rnd 3. In BLO (using the back loops from rnd 2) sc in each back loop around [6]

Rnd 4. Sc in each st around [6]

Fasten off the yarn, leaving a short tail of around 8-10 in. for attaching to the Body.

ASSEMBLY

1. Stitch the top edge of the Beak 2 rnds down from the bottom of the felt around the eyes.

2. Grab the Wattle and weave in the shorter tail. Weave the longer tail about 5 or 6 st toward the middle. Center the Wattle on the top row of the Beak and stitch it to the Beak, leaving the ends to hang free on either side. Use the Deep Red tail to embroider 2 diagonal lines going from the edges of the Beak to the outsides of the eyes.

3. Attach the Wings on either side of the Body on a diagonal with the tip of the Wing pointing toward the back. The top of the Wing should be around rnd 17.

4. Attach the tops of the Legs about 2 rnds from the bottom center of the Body, with the three-taloned side facing forward.

FUN FACT Although they're not married, Camilla and Gonzo's long-term relationship serves as the greatest example of true love between a chicken and ... whatever Gonzo is.

Rowlf the Dog!

Rowlf is not only the funniest piano-playing dog, but he's also the punniest. He's never met a pun he doesn't love and use ... over and over, no bones about it. A down-to-earth and lovable hound, Rowlf never shies away from a wisecrack even when he's the target. He studied piano under Madame Poochini at Ruff Barker's Obedience and Music School. Onstage, he's a lively, quick-witted, honky-tonk piano-playing songster. Backstage he's a wise advice-giver, a keen observer of life who likes to take it easy.

FUN FACT Rowlf was the first member of The Muppets to make it big in show business, booking regular commercials and late-night television appearances in the 1960s.

Rowlf the Dog

FINISHED MEASUREMENTS
Height: 9 in. / 23 cm
Width: 5 in. / 12.75 cm

YARN
Worsted weight (#4 medium) yarn, shown in Big Twist *Value* (100% acrylic, 380 yd. / 347 m per 6 oz. / 170 g skein)
Head/Body/Ears/Legs/Arms: Cinnamon
Face: Camel
Mouth/Nose: Black

HOOK
US F-5 / 3.75 mm hook

NOTIONS
• Pair of 6 mm plastic safety eyes
• White felt for eyes
• Polyester stuffing
• Tapestry needle
• Removable stitch markers

SPECIAL STITCHES
Back Loop Only (BLO): Work through back loop only
Pop3: Popcorn stitch with 3 DC

NOTES
The Mouth and Face are separate pieces that get crocheted together, the Body and Arms are also separate pieces that get crocheted together, so it is important to make them in order.

For more information on how to make Rowlf, including tips, step-by-step pictures, and videos, scan this QR code!

MOUTH

With Black, make a magic ring

Rnd 1. Sc 6 in ring [6]

Rnd 2. (Inc) x6 [12]

Rnd 3. (Sc, inc) x6 [18]

Rnd 4. (Sc 2, inc) x6 [24]

Rnd 5. (Sc 3, inc) x6 [30]

Rnd 6. (Sc 4, inc) x6 [36]

Fasten off the yarn and weave in the ends.

FACE

With Camel, make a magic ring

Rnd 1. Sc 6 in ring [6]

Rnd 2. (Inc) x6 [12]

Rnd 3. (Sc, inc) x6 [18]

Rnd 4. (Sc 2, inc) x6 [24]

Rnd 5. (Sc 3, inc) x6 [30]

Rnd 6. (Sc 4, inc) x6 [36]

Rnds 7–11. Sc in each st around [5 rnds of 36 st]

Rnd 12. *Grab the mouth and line it up with the Face, wrong sides together, so the next Camel st lines up with the last st that was made on the Mouth. Insert hook through both the Camel and Black st and crochet them together* sc 18, *work the rest of the rnd in the Camel st* sc 18 [36]

Insert safety eyes into white felt and trim to make a small egg shape around each eye, with the eye toward the smaller end. Insert the eye with the white felt. Insert the eyes with the felt in between rnds 7 and 8, around 4 st apart, centered above the Mouth.

Rnd 13. *Work into the Black st on the bottom half of the Mouth* sc18, *work the rest of the rnd in the Camel st* sc 18 [36]

Rnd 14. In BLO sc 18, in both loops sc 18 [36]

Rnds 15–16. Sc in each st around [2 rnds of 36 st]

Begin stuffing the Head—add just enough stuffing so that the Head keeps its shape without causing the Mouth to bulge:

Rnd 17. (Sc 4, dec) x6 [30]

Rnd 18. (Sc 3, dec) x6 [24]

Rnd 19. (Sc 2, dec) x6 [18]

Rnd 20. (Sc, dec) x6 [12]

Rnd 21. (Dec) x6 [6]

Fasten off the yarn, leaving a short tail around 6 in. long. Use your needle to weave the tail through the front loops of the last rnd and pull tight to close. Pull the tail to the inside of the Body and trim any excess.

HEAD

With Cinnamon, make a magic ring

Rnd 1. Sc 6 in ring [6]

Rnd 2. (Inc) x6 [12]

Rnd 3. (Sc, inc) x6 [18]

Rnd 4. (Sc 2, inc) x6 [24]

Rnd 5. (Sc 3, inc) x6 [30]

Rnd 6. (Sc 4, inc) x6 [36]

Rnds 7–14. Sc in each st around [8 rnds of 36 st]

Fasten off the yarn, leaving a long tail of around 20-22 in. for attaching to the Face.

NOSE

With Black, make a magic ring

Rnd 1. Sc 6 in ring [6]

Rnd 2. (Sc 2, sc 3 in the same st) x2 [10]

Rnd 3. Sc in each st around [10]

Fasten off the yarn, leaving a short tail of around 8-10 in. for attaching to the Face.

EARS (Make 2)

With Cinnamon, make a magic ring

Rnd 1. Sc 6 in ring [6]

Rnd 2. (Inc) x6 [12]

Rnd 3. (Sc, inc) x6 [18]

Rnds 4–6. Sc in each st around [3 rnds of 18 st]

Rnd 7. (Sc, dec) x6 [12]

Rnds 8–10. Sc in each st around [3 rnds of 12 st]

Rnd 11. Press the previous rnd together so the st line up and sc them together [6]

Fasten off the yarn, leaving a short tail of around 8-10 in. for attaching to the Head.

ARMS (Make 2)

With Cinnamon , make a magic ring

Rnd 1. Sc 6 in ring [6]

Rnd 2. (Inc) x6 [12]

Rnd 3. (Sc, inc) x6 [18]

Rnds 4–6. Sc in each st around [3 rnds of 18 st]

Rnd 7. Sc, pop3, sc 16 [18]

Rnd 8. Sc in each st around [18]

Rnd 9. (Sc 7, dec) x2 [16]

Rnds 10–13. Sc in each st around [4 rnds of 16 st]

Add stuffing to the hand; the rest of the Arm remains unstuffed:

Rnd 14. (Sc 2, dec) x4 [12]

Rnds 15–20. Sc in each st around [6 rnds of 12 st]

Rnd 21. (Sc 4, dec) x2 [10]

Rnd 22. Sc 3, press the previous rnd together so the st line up and sc them together [5]

Fasten off the yarn and weave in the ends.

BODY

With Cinnamon, make a magic ring

Rnd 1. Sc 6 in ring [6]

Rnd 2. (Inc) x6 [12]

Rnd 3. (Sc, inc) x6 [18]

Rnd 4. (Sc 2, inc) x6 [24]

Rnd 5. (Sc 3, inc) x6 [30]

Rnd 6. (Sc 4, inc) x6 [36]

Rnd 7. (Sc 5, inc) x6 [42]

Rnds 8–20. Sc in each st around [13 rnds of 42 st]

Rnd 21. *Grab one of the Arms and place it so the 5 st at the top line up with the next 5 st on the body and sc them together*, sc 16, *grab the other Arm and attach in the same manner as the first*, sc 16 [42 st with 2 arms]

Rnd 22. (Sc 3, dec) x8, sc 2 [34]

Fasten off the yarn, leaving a long tail of around 20-22 in. for attaching to the Head.

LEGS (MAKE 2)

With Cinnamon, make a magic ring

Rnd 1. Sc 6 in ring [6]

Rnd 2. (Sc 3 in the same st, inc, sc) x2 [12]

Rnd 3. Sc, (inc) x3, sc 3, (inc) x3, sc 2 [18]

Rnd 4. Sc 1, (sc, inc) x3, sc 3, (sc, inc) x3, sc 2 [24]

Rnd 5. Sc 2, (sc, inc) x3, sc 6, (sc, inc) x3, sc 4 [30]

Rnds 6–7. Sc in each st around [2 rnds of 30 st]

Rnd 8. Sc 2, (dec) x6, sc 16 [24]

Rnd 9. (Sc 2, dec) x6 [18]

Rnds 10–13. Sc in each st around [4 rnds of 18 st]

Rnd 14. (Sc 4, dec) x3 [15]

Rnds 15–17. Sc in each st around [3 rnds of 15 st]

Add stuffing to the foot; the rest of the Leg remains unstuffed.

Rnd 18. (Sc 3, dec) x3 [12]

Rnds 19–20. Sc in each st around [2 rnds of 12 st]

Rnd 21. Sc, press the top of the Leg together so the st line up and sc them together [6]

Fasten off the yarn, leaving a short tail of around 8-10 in. for attaching to the Body.

ASSEMBLY

1. Insert the Face into the Head so the back half is covered, and use the long tail to stitch the Head down.

2. Stuff the Nose and attach it to the center of the Face, directly above the Mouth.

3. Stuff the Body fully and attach it to the center of the underside of the Head. Be sure that the Head is positioned correctly so it sits nicely on top of the Body and the Arms are on either side.

4. Attach the Ears to the top of the Head, about 2 st apart, so they flop down on either side of the Head.

5. Attach the top of the Legs to the bottom of the Body so that they meet in the center; make sure the feet are facing forward.

Scooter!

Scooter, an enthusiastic go-getter who loves working in show business, acts as stage manager during most Muppet productions. He's usually the only one who knows what's supposed to happen next. Scooter remains calm longer than most of the other Muppets, but eventually he loses his cool and panics. Scooter likes being behind the scenes most of the time, but when the opportunity presents itself and the spotlight hits him, Scooter is always ready for showtime!

FUN FACT Scooter is one of the few Muppets who can get The Electric Mayhem on stage on time!

Scooter

FINISHED MEASUREMENTS
Height: 8 in. / 14 cm
Width: 4 in. / 10 cm

YARN
Worsted weight (#4 medium) yarn, shown in Big Twist *Value* (100% acrylic, 380 yd. / 347 m per 6 oz. / 170 g skein)
Head/Body: Varsity Gold
Mouth/Shoes: Varsity Red
Shirt/Jacket: Varsity Yellow
Pants: Denim
Shoes: White
Hair: Orange
Glasses: Black
Jacket: Light Green

HOOK
US F-5 / 3.75 mm hook

NOTIONS
- Polyester stuffing
- Pink, white, and black felt
- Tapestry needle
- Hot glue gun
- Removable stitch markers
- Black embroidery floss
- Embroidery needle

GAUGE
Gauge is not critical for this project. Ensure your stitches are tight so the stuffing won't show through.

SPECIAL STITCHES
Back Loop Only (BLO): Work through back loop only
Sc2tog: Single crochet 2 st together
Hdc2tog: Half double crochet 2 st together

NOTES
The Mouth, Head/Body, and Arms are separate pieces that get crocheted together, so it is important to make them in order.

For more information on how to make Scooter, including tips, step-by-step pictures, and videos, scan this QR code!

MOUTH

With Varsity Red, make a magic ring

Rnd 1. Sc 8 in ring [8]

Rnd 2. (Inc, sc, sc 3 in the same st, sc) x2 [14]

Rnd 3. (Inc, sc 3, sc 3 in the same st, sc 2) x2 [20]

Rnd 4. Sc, inc, sc 4, sc 3 in the same st, sc 4, inc, sc 4, sc 3 in the same st, sc 3 [26]

Rnd 5. Sc, inc, sc 6, sc 3 in the same st, sc 6, inc, sc *place a stitch marker in the last st made*, sc 4, sc 3 in the same st, sc 4 [32]

Fasten off the yarn and set aside for now.

ARMS (Make 2)

With Varsity Gold, make a magic ring

Rnd 1. Sc 6 in ring [6]

Rnd 2. (Inc) x6 [12]

Rnds 3–4. Sc in each st around [2 rnds of 12 st]

Rnd 5. (Sc, dec) x4, on the last st of the rnd change to Varsity Yellow [8]

Rnds 6–17. Sc in each st around, *after a few rnds, add a small amount of stuffing to the hands only) [12 rnds of 8 st]

Rnd 18. Press the previous rnd together so the st line up and sc them together [4]

Fasten off the yarn and weave in the ends.

HEAD AND BODY

With Varsity Gold, make a magic ring

Rnd 1. Sc 8 in ring [8]

Rnd 2. (Inc, sc, sc 3 in the same st, sc) x2 [14]

Rnds 3–4. Sc in each st around [2 rnds of 14 st]

Rnd 5. (Inc, sc 3, sc 3 in the same st, sc 2) x2 [20]

Rnds 6–8. Sc in each st around [3 rnds of 20 st]

Rnd 9. Sc, inc, sc 4, sc 3 in the same st, sc 4, inc, sc 4, sc 3 in the same st, sc 3 [26]

Rnd 10. Sc, inc, sc 6, sc 3 in the same st, sc 6, inc, sc 5, sc 3 in the same st, sc 4 [32]

Rnd 11. Sc in each st around [32]

Rnd 12. Sc, *grab the Mouth and line it up with the Head, wrong sides together, so the next Varsity Gold st lines up with the st that was marked on rnd 5 of the Mouth. Insert hook through both the Varsity Gold and Varsity Red st and crochet them together* sc 18, *work the rest of the rnd in only the Varsity Gold st* sc 13 [32]

Rnd 13. Inc, *work into the Varsity Red st on the bottom half of the Mouth* sc 14, *work the rest of the rnd in the Varsity Gold st*, inc, sc 12 [30]

Rnd 14. Sc 2, in BLO sc 14, in both loops sc 14 [30]

Rnd 15. Sc in each st around [30]

Rnd 16. (Sc 3, dec) x6 [24]

Begin stuffing the Head—add just enough stuffing so that the Head keeps its shape without causing the Mouth to bulge:

Rnd 17. (Sc 2, dec) x6 [18]

Rnd 18. (Sc, dec) x6, on the last st of the rnd change to Varsity Yellow [12]

Rnd 19. (Sc, inc) x6 [18]

Rnd 20. Sc in each st around [18]

Rnd 21. (Sc 2, inc) x6 [24]

Rnd 22. Sc 2, *Grab one of the Arms and place it so the 4 st at the top line up with the next 4 st on the body and sc them together*, sc 8, *grab the other Arm and attach in the same manner as the first*, sc 6 [24 st with 2 Arms]

Rnds 23–24. Sc in each st around [2 rnds of 24 st]

Rnd 25. (Sc 3, inc) x6 [30]

Rnds 26–28. Sc in each st around [3 rnds of 30 st]

Rnd 29. (Sc 4, inc) x6 [36]

Rnd 30. Sc in each st around, on the last st of the rnd change to Denim yarn [36]

Rnds 31–32. Sc in each st around [2 rnds of 36 st]

Rnd 33. (Sc 4, dec) x6 [30]

Finish stuffing the Head and begin stuffing the Body. Continue stuffing as you work the remaining rnds.

Rnd 34. (Sc 3, dec) x6 [24]

Rnd 35. (Sc 2, dec) x6 [18]

Rnd 36. (Sc, dec) x6 [12]

Rnd 37. (Dec) x6 [6]

Fasten off the yarn, leaving a short tail around 6 in. long. Use your needle to weave the tail through the front loops of the last rnd and pull tight to close. Pull the tail to the inside of the Body and trim any excess.

LEGS (Make 2)

With White, make a magic ring

Rnd 1. Sc 6 in ring [6]

Rnd 2. (Sc 3 in the same st, inc, sc) x2 [12]

Rnd 3. Sc, (inc) x3, sc 3, (inc) x3, sc 2 [18]

Rnd 4. Sc in each st around, on the last st of the rnd change to Varsity Red [18]

Rnd 5. Sc in each st around [18]

Rnd 6. (Dec) x4, sc 10 [14]

Rnd 7. (Dec) x2, sc 10, on the last st of the rnd change to Denim [12]

Rnds 8–17. Sc in each st around [10 rnds of 12 st]

Add stuffing to the foot; the rest of the Leg remains unstuffed.

Rnd 18. (Sc 4, dec) x2 [10]

Rnd 19. Press the previous rnd together so the st line up and sc them together [5]

Fasten off the yarn, leaving a short tail of around 8-10 in. for attaching to the Body.

EARS (Make 2)

With Varsity Gold

Row 1. Ch 2, in the second ch from the hook sc 3 in the same space, ch 1 but do not turn [3]

Row 2. Continue around the bottom of the ear sc 2 [2]

Fasten off the yarn, leaving a short tail of around 8-10 in. for attaching to the Body.

HAIR

With Orange, make a magic ring

Rnd 1. Sc 5 in ring [5]

Rnd 2. (Ch 4, starting in the second ch from the hook sl st 3, ch 5, starting in the second ch from the hook sl st 3, sl st on ring, ch 4, starting in the second ch from the hook sl st 3, sl st on the ring) x2, ch 4, starting in the second ch from the hook sl st 3, sl st on the ring [7 short locks of hair]

Fasten off the yarn, leaving a short tail of around 8-10 in. for attaching to the Head.

JACKET

Row 1. In Light Green ch 31, starting in the back bump of the second ch from the hook sc 30 in the back bumps of the ch, ch 1 and turn [30]

Rows 2–13. Sc in each st across, ch 1 and turn [12 rows of 30 st]

Row 14. Sc 4, ch 7, skip 7 st, sc 8, ch 7, skip 7 st, sc 4, ch 1 and turn [30 st with 2 armholes]

Row 15. Sc in each st and ch across, ch 1 and turn [30]

Row 16. (Sc2tog, sc 3) x3, (sc 3, sc2tog) x3 ch 1 [24]

Row 17. *Side 1*: Do not turn, continue down the side hdc 14, (hdc 2, ch 1, hdc 2 in the last st on the side

Bottom: Continue around the bottom of the Jacket, hdc, change to Varsity Yellow, hdc 26, change to Light Green, hdc, (hdc 2, ch 1, hdc 2) in the last st on the bottom

Side 2: Continue around to the other side of the Jacket, hdc 14 ch 2

Top: Continue around to the top of the Jacket, (hdc2tog, hdc 2) x3, (hdc 2, hdc2tog) x3

Fasten off the yarn and weave in the ends.

JACKET SLEEVES (Make 2)

Rnd 1. Join Light Green to the corner of one of the armholes, sc 14 around the armhole [14]

Rnds 2–11. Sc in each st around, on the | last st of the rnd change to Varsity Yellow [10 rnds of 14 st]

Rnd 12. Hdc 14 [14]

Fasten off the yarn and weave in the end.

ASSEMBLY

1. Cut out 2 small circles of white felt, and 2 slightly larger circles of black felt. Stack the white circles centered on top of the black circles and use an embroidery needle with black embroidery floss to stitch a small dot in the center, forming a pupil and attaching the felt circles together.

2. Embroider the glasses with Black yarn and your tapestry needle, make a straight line that goes from the side of the Head between rnds 7 and 8 and continues all the way to the other side of the Head.

3. Use a hot glue gun to glue the eyes to the front of the face, about 1 sc apart, centered on the glasses line from step 2.

4. Stitch the Ears vertically on either side of the face, so the top lines up with the glasses.

5. Attach the Hair to the top of the Head by stitching down the magic ring portion, leaving the locks of Hair loose.

6. Stitch the Legs to the underside of the Body, slightly toward the front and about 2 st away from each other, with the feet facing forward.

7. Pull the Jacket on and close the front so the left side overlaps the right side. Use a strand of Varsity Yellow to sew the front of the Jacket closed in a dotted line, from the bottom up, giving the appearance of yellow buttons. Fasten off the yarn and weave in the ends.

8. Cut a small heart shape out of pink felt for the tongue and use a hot glue gun to attach it inside of the mouth.

Sam Eagle!

Sam has a fondness for the spotlight, usually to talk about patriotism, decency, and America. Despite his disdain for The Muppets' frivolous nonsense and inspired silliness, Sam sticks around for every single moment of it. Kermit understands the need to have Sam around, and actually tries to address Sam's concerns. That's because Sam sets a high moral standard for The Muppets, which The Muppets never ever come close to achieving.

FUN FACT Sam Eagle's hobbies include only the most patriotic handicrafts: needlepoint, quilting, and crochet.

Sam Eagle

FINISHED MEASUREMENTS

Height: 8 in. / 20.3 cm
Width: 4.5 in. / 11.5 cm

YARN

Worsted weight (#4 medium) yarn, shown in Big Twist *Value* (100% acrylic, 380 yd. / 347 m per 6 oz. / 170 g skein)
Head and Body/Beak/Lower Lip/Wings/Tail: Cornflower Blue
Feet: Varsity Gold
Eyebrow: Black

HOOK

US F-5 / 3.75 mm hook

NOTIONS

- Pair of 9 mm black plastic safety eyes
- Polyester stuffing
- Tapestry needle
- Pet brush or comb
- Removable stitch markers

GAUGE

Gauge is not critical for this project. Ensure your stitches are tight so the stuffing won't show through.

SPECIAL STITCHES

Back Loop Only (BLO): Work through back loop only
Front Loop Only (FLO): Work through front loop only
Picot (picot): Ch 3, sc into the back bump of first ch made

For more information on how to make Sam Eagle, including tips, step-by-step pictures, and videos, scan this QR code!

HEAD AND BODY

With Cornflower Blue, make a magic ring

Rnd 1. Sc 6 in ring [6]

Rnd 2. (Inc) x6 [12]

Rnd 3. (Sc, inc) x6 [18]

Rnd 4. (Sc 2, inc) x6 [24]

Rnd 5. (Sc 3, inc) x6, on the last st of the rnd change to Black yarn [30]

Rnds 6–7. Sc 11, change to Cornflower Blue yarn, sc 19

Rnds 8–23. Sc in each st around [16 rnds of 30 st]

Insert safety eyes into white felt and trim to make a small half circle around each eye; the safety eye should be closer to one side of the half circle and the two should mirror each other. Insert the eye with the felt in between rnds 8 and 9, about 5 st apart, and with the flat side of the half circle of felt on top, lining up with the Black st from rnds 6 and 7.

Rnd 24. (Sc 4, inc) x6 [36]

Rnd 25. (Sc 5, inc) x6 [42]

Rnds 26–33. Sc in each st around [8 rnds of 42 st]

Rnd 34. (Sc 5, dec) x6 [36]

Rnds 35–38. Sc in each st around [4 rnds of 36 st]

Begin stuffing the Head and Body fully, continue stuffing as you go:

Rnd 39. (Sc 4, dec) x6 [30]

Rnds 40–43. Sc in each st around [4 rnds of 30 st]

Rnd 44. (Sc 3, dec) x6 [24]

Rnd 45. (Sc 2, dec) x6 [18]

Rnd 46. (Sc, dec) x6 [12]

Rnd 47. (Dec) x6 [6]

Fasten off the yarn, leaving a short tail around 6 in. Use your needle to weave the tail through the front loops of the last rnd and pull tight to close. Pull the tail to the inside of the Body and trim any excess.

BEAK

With Cornflower Blue, make a magic ring

Rnd 1. Sc 4 in ring [4]

Rnd 2. Sc, (inc) x2, sc [6]

Rnd 3. Sc 2, (inc) x2, sc 2 [8]

Rnd 4. Sc 3, (inc) x2, sc 3 [10]

Rnd 5. Sc 4, (inc) x2, sc 4 [12]

Rnd 6. (Sc, inc) x6 [18]

Rnd 7. In BLO sl st 9, in both loops hdc 9 [18]

Rnd 8. In FLO from rnd 6 sc 9, through both loops hdc 9 [18]

Rnd 9. Sc in each st around [18]

Fasten off the yarn, leaving a short tail of around 8-10 in. for attaching to the Head.

LOWER LIP

With Cornflower Blue

Row 1. Ch 2, sc 3 in the second ch from the hook, ch 1 and turn [3]

Row 2. (Inc) x3 [6]

Fasten off the yarn, leaving a short tail of around 8-10 in. for attaching to the Head.

Rnd 15. (Sc 2, inc) x6 [24]

Rnds 16–17. Sc in each st around [2 rnds of 24 st]

Rnd 18. (Sc 2, dec) x6 [18]

Rnds 19–20. Sc in each st around [2 rnds of 18 st]

Rnd 21. (Sc, dec) x6 [12]

Rnd 22. Sc in each st around [12]

Rnd 23. Sc, press the previous rnd together so the st line up and sc them together [6]

Fasten off the yarn, leaving a short tail of around 8-10 in. for attaching to the Body.

TAIL

With Cornflower Blue, make a magic ring

Rnd 1. Sc 6 in ring [6]

Rnd 2. (Sc 2, inc) x2 [8]

Rnd 3. (Sc 3, inc) x2 [10]

Rnd 4. (Sc 4, inc) x2 [12]

Rnds 5–6. Sc in each st around [2 rnds of 12 st]

Rnd 7. (Sc, inc) x6 [18]

Rnds 8–9. Sc in each st around [2 rnds of 18 st]

Rnd 10. Press the previous rnd together so the st line up and sc them together, turn [9]

Rnd 11. (Picot, skip 1 st, sl st) x4, picot, sl st [5 picot stitches]

Fasten off the yarn, leaving a short tail of around 8-10 in. for attaching to the Body.

WINGS (Make 2)

With Cornflower Blue, make a magic ring

Rnd 1. Sc 6 in ring [6]

Rnd 2. Sc 2, (inc) x2, sc 2 [8]

Rnd 3. Sc 3, (inc) x2, sc 3 [10]

Rnd 4. Sc 4, (inc) x2, sc 4 [12]

Rnd 5. Sc in each st around [12]

Rnd 6. Sc 5, (inc) x2, sc 5 [14]

Rnd 7. Sc in each st around [14]

Rnd 8. Sc 6, (inc) x2, sc 6 [16]

Rnd 9. Sc in each st around [16]

Rnd 10. Sc 7, (inc) x2, sc 7 [18]

Rnds 11–14. Sc in each st around [4 rnds of 18 st]

LEGS (Make 2)

With Varsity Gold, make a magic ring

Rnd 1. Sc 6 in ring [6]

Rnd 2. In FLO sl st, ch 5, starting in the second ch from the hook sc 4, sl st 2, (ch 5, starting in the second ch from the hook sc 4, sl st) x3 [3 talons on the front of the foot, 1 talon on the back]

Rnd 3. BLO (using the back loops from rnd 2): Sc in each back loop around [6]

Rnds 4–6. Sc in each st around, in the last st of rnd 6 change to Cornflower Blue, [3 rnds of 6 st]

Rnd 7. (Inc) x6 [12]

Rnd 8. (Sc, inc) x6 [18]

Rnds 9–10. Sc in each st around [2 rnds of 18 st]

Rnd 11. (Sc, dec) x6 [12]

Rnd 12. Sc 5 (to get the proper alignment), press the previous rnd together so the st line up and sc them together [6]

Fasten off the yarn, leaving a short tail of around 8-10 in. for attaching to the Body.

ASSEMBLY

1. Cut several 3 in. strands of Black yarn. Using a Lark's Head knot, attach the strands to the eyebrow. (When attaching the strands be sure that your hook is always pointed to the bottom of the Head when first inserted. This will ensure that the knot is hidden.) Use a pet brush or comb to brush out the fibers of the yarn and trim to the desired length: around .25-.5 in.

2. Stuff the Beak, making sure to get stuffing all the way to the tip, then attach to the center of the face with the tip pointed down, spanning rnds 10-16, right beneath the eyes.

3. Stitch the flat side of the Lower Lip in a curve underneath the Beak, so that the top of the Lip is touching the underside of the Beak.

4. Attach the top edge of the Wings on either side of the Body. Angle them so they point slightly forward and with the top corner about 4 or 5 rnds down from the bottom of the Lower Lip.

5. Line up the Legs on either side of the Body, with the 3-taloned side of the foot facing forward, and so the color change from Varsity Gold to Cornflower Blue lines up with the bottom of the Body. Stitch along the top edge of the Leg and then continue to stitch down the side, across the bottom of the Cornflower Blue section and back up the other side.

6. Stitch the point of the Tail to the center back of the Body, so it lines up with the tops of the Legs, leaving the rest of the Tail unattached.

7. Cut a great deal of 4 in. strands of Cornflower Blue yarn. Attach them using a Lark's Head knot. (When attaching the strands be sure that your hook is always pointed to the bottom of the Body when first inserted. This will ensure that the knot is hidden.)

Head: Attach strands along the same rnd as the top of the Beak, starting at the side and continuing around the back of the Head to the other side.

Collar: Attach 2 strands at once to give a fuller look. Attach them in a straight line around the neck, 2 rnds down from the bottom of the Lower Lip.

Wings: Attach 2 strands at once on the wings as well. Attach the strands to the outside of the Wings, and staggered to give a patchy look that will resemble ruffled feathers when finished.

8. Use pet brush to brush out all of the strands until they are completely fuzzy and then trim to desired length.

Head: Trim to about 1 in. long and brush them straight down.

Collar: Trim to about 1-1.25 in. long and brush straight down.

Wings: Trim each segment to about .5 in. long and brush straight down.

Pepé the King Prawn!

Pepé is a schemer, a charmer, and an unrelenting opportunist. (He is not a shrimp! Never say that word!) Born off the coast of Spain, Pepé discovered that show business was a good way to avoid becoming part of a seafood buffet. He also learned that show business is a great way to make the monies. Pepé likes being part of The Muppets, and has endless ideas for making them more "successful." Fortunately, Kermit (whom Pepé calls "Karmin") is too smart to go along with many of Pepé's schemes. It doesn't stop this hot and spicy prawn from trying, okay?

FUN FACT Pepé is one of the most renowned dancers at The Muppets Theatre, showcasing his abilities in everything from ballet to samba.

Pepé the King Prawn

FINISHED MEASUREMENTS
Height: 9.5 in. / 24 cm
Width: 6 in. / 15.25 cm

YARN
Worsted weight (#4 medium) yarn shown in Red Heart *Super Saver* (100% acrylic, 364 yd. / 333 m per 7 oz. / 198 g skein)
Arms/Head/Body: Carrot

Worsted weight (#4 medium) yarn, shown in Big Twist *Value* (100% acrylic, 380 yd. / 347 m per 6 oz. / 170 g skein)
Eyes/Tooth: White
Mouth/Sweater/Eyelid: Black
Eyelids/Hair: Varsity Red
Lower Lip: Cream
Necklace: Varsity Gold

HOOK
US F-5 / 3.75 mm hook
US G-6 / 4 mm hook

NOTIONS
- Pair of 6 mm black plastic safety eyes
- Pink felt for tongue
- Polyester stuffing
- Tapestry needle
- Hot glue gun
- Removable stitch markers

GAUGE
Gauge is not critical for this project. Ensure your stitches are tight so the stuffing won't show through.

SPECIAL STITCHES
Back Loop Only (BLO): Work through back loop only
Front Loop Only (FLO): Work through front loop only
Sc2tog: Single crochet 2 stitches together

NOTE
The Mouth, Arms, and Head/Body are separate pieces that get crocheted together, so it is important to make them in order.

For more information on how to make Pepé, including tips, step-by-step pictures, and videos, scan this QR code!

MOUTH

With 3.75 mm hook and Black, make a magic ring

Rnd 1. Sc 6 in ring [6]

Rnd 2. (Sc 3 in the same st, inc, sc) x2 [12]

Rnd 3. Sc, (inc) x3, sc 3, (inc) x3, sc 2 [18]

Rnd 4. Sc 1, (sc, inc) x3, sc 3, (sc, inc) x3, sc 2 [24]

Put a removable stitch marker in the second to last stitch made. Fasten off the yarn and weave in the ends.

ARMS (Make 4)

With 3.75 mm hook and Carrot, make a magic ring

Rnd 1. Sc 6 in ring [6]

Rnd 2. In FLO sl st, (ch 3, starting in the second ch from the hook sc 2, sl st to the next st on the circle) x3, sc 3 through both loops [6 st with 3 fingers]

Rnd 3. In BLO (using the back loops from rnd 2) sc 3, sc 3 through both loops [6]

Rnds 4–14. Sc in each st around [11 rnds of 6 st]

Rnd 15. Press the previous rnd together so the st line up and sc them together [3]

Fasten off the yarn and weave in the ends.

HEAD AND BODY

With 3.75 mm hook and Carrot, make a magic ring

Rnd 1. Sc 6 in ring [6]

Rnd 2. (Inc) x6 [12]

Rnd 3. (Sc, inc) x6 [18]

Rnds 4–6. Sc in each st around [3 rnds of 18 st]

Rnd 7. *Grab the Mouth and line it up with the Head, wrong sides together, so the marked st lines up with the next st on the Head: Insert hook through both the Carrot and Black st and crochet them together* sc 10, *work the rest of the rnd in the Carrot st* sc 8 [18]

Rnd 8. *Work into the Black st on the bottom half of the mouth* sc 14, *work the rest of the rnd in the Carrot st* sc 8 [22]

Rnd 9. Sc 2, dec, sc, (dec) x2, sc, dec, sc 10 [18]

Rnds 10–15. Sc in each st around [6 rnds of 18 st]

Begin stuffing the Head, but do not stuff the lower jaw.

Rnd 16. (Sc 2, inc) x6 [24]

Rnd 17. (Sc 3, inc) x6 [30]

Rnd 18. (Sc 4, inc) x6 [36]

Rnd 19. *Grab one of the Arms and place it so the 3 st at the top line up with the next 3 st on the Body and sc them together*, sc 15, *grab the other Arm and attach in the same manner as the first*, sc 15 [36 st with 2 Arms]

Rnds 20–21. Sc in each st around [2 rnds of 36 st]

Rnd 22. Sc, *Grab one of the Arms and place it so the 3 st at the top line up with the next 3 st on the Body and sc them together*, sc 15, *grab the other Arm and attach in the same manner as the first*, sc 14 [36 st with 2 Arms]

Rnds 23–27. Sc in each st around [5 rnds of 36 st]

Rnd 28. (Sc 4, dec) x6 [30]

Begin stuffing the Body fully and continue stuffing as you go.

Rnd 29. (Sc 3, dec) x6 [24]

Rnd 30. (Sc 2, dec) x6 [18]

Rnd 31. (Sc, dec) x6 [12]

Rnd 32. (Dec) x6 [6]

Fasten off the yarn, leaving a short tail around 6 in. Use your needle to weave the tail through the front loops of the last rnd and pull tight to close. Pull the tail to the inside of the Body and trim any excess.

BELLY PANEL

With 3.75 mm and Varsity Gold

Rnd 1. Ch 7, starting in the back bump of the second ch from the hook sc 6, ch 1 and turn [6]

Rnd 2. Inc, sc 4, inc, ch 1 and turn [8]

Rnd 3. Inc, sc 6, inc, ch 1 and turn [10]

Rnds 4–13. Sc in each st across, ch 1 and turn [10 rows of 10 st]

Rnd 14. Sc2tog, sc 6, sc2tog, ch 1 and turn [8]

Rnd 15. Sc2tog, sc 4, sc2tog, ch 1 and turn [6]

Rnd 16. Sc2tog, sc 2, sc2tog, ch 1 and turn [4]

Rnds 17–20. Sc in each st across, ch 1 and turn [4 rows of 4 st]

Rnd 21. Sc around the entire perimeter of the panel

Side 1: Continue down the side, sc 20

Bottom: Continue along the bottom, sc 6

Side 2: Continue along the other side, sc 20 [50]

Fasten off the yarn, leaving a long tail around 30 in. for attaching to the body.

EYES (Make 2)

With 3.75 mm hook and White, make a magic ring

Rnd 1. Sc 6 in ring [6]

Rnd 2. (Sc, inc) x3 [9]

Rnd 3. Sc in each st around [9]

Insert safety eye in between rnds 1 and 2.

Fasten off the yarn, leaving a short tail around 8-10 in. for attaching to the Head. The back of the safety eye should help the Eye keep its shape, but if you'd like to add a small amount of stuffing, feel free to do so.

EYELIDS (Make 1 Right and 1 Left)

With 3.75 mm and Carrot

Row 1. Ch 2, sc 3 in the second ch from the hook, ch 1 and turn [3]

Row 2. (Inc) x3, ch 1 and turn [6]

Row 3. (Sc, inc) x3, on the last st of the row change to Black yarn, ch 1 and turn [9]

Row 4. *Pepé's Right Eyelid*: In BLO skip the first st, sl st 7, make 2 sl st in the last st of the row

Pepé's Left Eyelid: In BLO sl st 9 [9]

Fasten off each color of yarn, leaving a short tail of around 8-10 in. of each color for attaching to the Head.

ANTENNAE (Make 2)

With 3.75 mm hook and Carrot

Ch 13, starting in the second ch from the hook sl st 12 [12]

Fasten off the yarn, leaving a short tail of around 4 in. for attaching to the Head.

LOWER LIP

With 3.75 mm hook and Cream

Ch 14, starting in the second ch from the hook hdc 13 [13]

Fasten off the yarn, leaving a tail around 20 in. long for attaching to the Mouth.

TOOTH

With 3.75 mm hook and White

Ch 2, sl st in the second ch from the hook [1]

Fasten off the yarn, leaving a short tail of around 4 in. for attaching to the Mouth.

LEGS (Make 2)

With 3.75 mm hook and Carrot, make a magic ring

Rnd 1. Sc 6 in ring [6]

Rnd 2. (Sc 3 in the same st, inc, sc) x2 [12]

Rnd 3. Sc, (inc) x3, sc 3, (inc) x3, sc 2 [18]

Rnd 4. Sc in each st around [18]

Rnd 5. (Dec) x4, sc 10 [14]

Rnd 6. (Dec) x2, sc 10 [12]

Rnd 7. (Sc, dec) x4 [8]

Rnds 8–18. Sc in each st around [11 rnds of 8 st]

Rnd 19. Sc, press the top of the Leg together so the st line up and sc them together [3]

Fasten off the yarn, leaving a short tail of around 8-10 in. for attaching to the Body.

TURTLENECK

The turtleneck is made from the bottom up and in joining rnds. At the end of each rnd, sl st into the first st of the rnd and ch 1. The next rnd begins in the same space as the sl st.

With 4 mm hook and Black

Rnd 1. Ch 36, make sure the ch is not twisted and sl st into the first ch made and ch 1

Rnds 2–8. Sc in each around, sl st join and ch 1 [7 rnds of 36 st]

Rnd 9. Sc 6, ch 6, skip 6 st, sc 12, ch 6, skip 6 st, sc 6, sl st join and ch 1 [36 st with 2 armholes]

Rnd 10. Sc in each st and ch around, sl st join and ch 1 [36]

Rnds 11–12. Sc in each st around [2 rnds of 36 st]

Rnd 13. Sc 6, ch 6, skip 6 st, sc 12, ch 6, skip 6 st, sc 6, sl st join and ch 1 [36 st with 2 armholes]

Rnd 14. Sc in each st and ch around [36]

Rnd 15. (Sc 4, dec) x6 [30]

Rnd 16. (Sc 3, dec) x6 [24]

Rnd 17. (Sc 2, dec) x6 [18]

Rnd 18. In BLO sc in each st around [18]

Rnds 19–22. Sc in each st around [4 rnds of 18 st]

Fasten off the yarn and weave in the tails.

SLEEVES (Make 4)

Rnd 1. Join yarn to the corner of one of the armholes, sc 12 around the armhole [12]

Rnds 2–14. Sc in each st around [13 rnds of 12 st]

Fasten off the yarn and weave in the ends.

NECKLACE

With 3.75 mm hook and Varsity Gold

Ch 30 [30]

Fasten off the yarn, leaving a short tail of around 4 in. for attaching to the Body.

ASSEMBLY

1. Attach the Eyes to the Head, one round up from the top lip of the Mouth, with the safety eyes set toward the center of the face.

2. Starting with the Black yarn tail, attach Pepé's Left Eyelid to the Eye, about 1 rnd up from the safety eye, so the back of the Eyelid touches the Head, weave in the ends. Use the Carrot tail to stitch the back of the Eyelid to the face, around the Eye, weave in the ends.

3. Repeat step 2 with Pepé's Right Eyelid.

4. Attach the Antennae to the top of the Head, directly behind the Eyelids.

5. Attach the Lower Lip around the bottom of the Mouth so it covers the color change. Be sure to stitch both the bottom and top edges down; weave in the ends.

6. Attach the Tooth to the lower jaw, directly behind the Lip, on Pepé's right side.

7. Attach the Belly Panel so that the narrow end lines up with the center of the Lower Lip and stitch down around all edges.

8. Attach the top of the Legs to the bottom of the Body so that they meet in the center; make sure the feet are facing forward.

9. Pull the Turtleneck on. You may need to use your crochet hook to reach inside the sleeves and pull the Arms out.

10. Attach the Necklace to the center back of the Turtleneck at the base of the neck, leaving the rest of the Necklace unattached.

Rizzo the Rat!

Rizzo defines the phrase "street smart." He grew up on—or rather, under—the streets of Brooklyn. A wise guy who knows how to land on his feet, find a meal, and avoid getting caught, Rizzo never lets anything stand between him and survival. He's an entrepreneur who never says no to an opportunity. That said, he loves being part of The Muppets and would do anything to help Kermit. Rizzo is a best pal to Gonzo, whom he finds odd but lovable.

FUN FACT Rizzo prefers to spend life surrounded by his friends and his food, and is never far from a stash of jelly beans.

Rizzo the Rat

FINISHED MEASUREMENTS
Height: 9 in. / 23 cm
Width: 4.5 in. / 11.5 cm

YARN
Worsted weight (#4 medium) yarn shown in Red Heart *Super Saver* (100% acrylic, 364 yd. / 333 m per 7 oz. / 198 g skein)
Body/Head/Arms/Legs: Espresso

Worsted weight (#4 medium) yarn, shown in Big Twist *Value* (100% acrylic, 380 yd. / 347 m per 6 oz. / 170 g skein)
Eyes/Tooth/Shirt: White
Mouth/Jacket: Varsity Red
Eyelids: Soft Gray
Ears: Mushroom
Sleeves: Cream
Nose/Cuffs: Black

HOOK
US F-5 / 3.75 mm hook

NOTIONS
- Pair of 6 mm black plastic safety eyes
- Pink felt for tongue
- Polyester stuffing
- Tapestry needle
- Hot glue gun
- Blush or pink felt for inside the Ears
- Removable stitch markers

GAUGE
Gauge is not critical for this project. Ensure your stitches are tight so the stuffing won't show through

SPECIAL STITCHES
Back Loop Only (BLO): Work through back loop only
Front Loop Only (FLO): Work through front loop only
Sc2tog: Single crochet 2 stitches together

NOTES
The Mouth, Head/Body, and Arms are separate pieces that get crocheted together, so it is important to make them in order.

For more information on how to make Rizzo, including tips, step-by-step pictures, and videos, scan this QR code!

MOUTH

With Varsity Red

Ch 4, starting in the second ch from the hook sc 2, sc 3 in the same stitch, continue around to the other side of the ch, skip 1 st, hdc 1, dc 1, ch 1 and continue around the bottom (inc) x2 [11]

Fasten off the yarn and weave in the ends.

ARMS (Make 2)

With Espresso, make a magic ring

Rnd 1. Sc 8 in ring [8]

Rnds 2–4. Sc in each st around [3 rnds of 8 st]

Rnd 5. (Sc 2, dec) x2 [6]

Rnds 6–14. Sc in each st around, *after a few rnds, add a small amount of stuffing to the hands only*, on the last st of rnd 14 change to White yarn [9 rnds of 6 st]

Rnds 15–18. Sc in each st around [4 rnds of 6 st]

Rnd 19. Press the previous rnd together so the st line up and sc them together [3]

Fasten off the yarn and weave in the ends.

HEAD AND BODY

With Espresso, make a magic ring

Rnd 1. Sc 6 in ring [6]

Rnd 2. (Inc) x6 [12]

Rnd 3. (Sc, inc) x6 [18]

Rnd 4. (Sc 2, inc) x6 [24]

Rnds 5–8. Sc in each st around [4 rnds of 24 st]

Rnd 9. Sc 10, *grab the Mouth and place it on the outside of the Head so that the 4 st along the bottom line up with the next 4 st on the Head and sc them together*, sc 10 [24]

Rnd 10. Sc 10, sc 3 up the side of the Mouth, (sc, ch 2, sc) in the corner, sc 3 down the other side of the Mouth, sc 10 [30]

Rnd 11. Sc 10, in BLO sc 4, skip the ch 2 space, sc 4, through both loops sc 10 [30]

Rnd 12. Sc 10, (dec) x4, sc 10 [24]

Rnd 13. (Sc 2, dec) x6 [18]

Rnd 14. (Sc, dec) x6 [12]

Rnds 15–18. Sc in each st around [4 rnds of 12 st]

Rnd 19. (Sc, inc) x6, on the last st of the rnd change to White yarn [18]

Rnd 20. (Sc 2, inc) x6 [24]

Rnd 21. (Sc 3, inc) x6 [30]

Rnd 22. Sc 9, *grab one of the Arms and place it so the 3 st at the top line up with the next 3 st on the Body and sc them together*, sc 12, *grab the second Arm and attach in the same manner as the first*, sc 3 [30 with 2 Arms attached]

Rnds 23–26. Sc in each st around [4 rnds of 30 st]

Rnd 27. (Sc 4, inc) x6 [36]

Rnd 28. Sc in each st around, on the last st of the rnd change to Espresso [36]

Rnd 29. In BLO sc in each st around [36]

Rnd 30. (Sc 5, inc) x6 [42]

Rnds 31–32. Sc in each st around [2 rnds of 42 st]

Rnd 33. (Sc 5, dec) x6 [36]

Begin stuffing the Head and Body and continue stuffing as you go

Rnd 34. (Sc 4, dec) x6 [30]

Rnd 35. (Sc 3, dec) x6 [24]

Rnd 36. (Sc 2, dec) x6 [18]

Rnd 37. (Sc, dec) x6 [12]

Rnd 38. (Dec) x6 [6]

Fasten off the yarn, leaving a short tail around 6 in. Use your needle to weave the tail through the front loops of the last rnd and pull tight to close. Pull the tail to the inside of the Body and trim any excess.

EYES (Make 2)

With White, make a magic ring

Rnd 1. Sc 6 in ring [6]

Rnd 2. (Sc, inc) x3 [9]

Insert safety eye in the center of the magic ring

Rnd 3. (Sc, dec) x3 [6]

Fasten off the yarn, leaving a short tail around 8-10 in. for attaching to the Head. The back of the safety eye should help the Eye keep its shape, but if you'd like to add a small amount of stuffing, feel free to do so.

EYELIDS (Make 2)

With Soft Gray, make a magic ring

Rnd 1. Sc 6 in ring [6]

Rnd 2. (Sc, inc) x3 [9]

Fasten off the yarn, leaving a short tail of around 8-10 in. for attaching to the Eyes.

NOSE

With Espresso, make a magic ring

Rnd 1. Sc 4 in ring [4]

Rnd 2. Sc, (inc) x2, sc [6]

Rnd 3. Sc 2, (inc) x2, sc 2 [8]

Rnd 4. Sc 3, (inc) x2, sc 3 [10]

Rnd 5. Sc 4, (inc) x2, sc 4 [12]

Rnd 6. Sc in each st around [12]

Rnd 7. Sc 3, *this will be the new start of your rnd*

Rnd 8. Hdc 6, in BLO sl st 6 [12]

Rnd 9. Inc, sc 4, inc, in the front loops from rnd 8 sc 6 [14]

Rnd 10. Inc, sc 4, inc, in BLO sl st 8 [16]

Rnd 11. Inc, sc 6, inc, in the front loops from rnd 10 sc 8 [18]

Rnd 12. Sc in each st around [18]

Fasten off the yarn, leaving a short tail of around 8-10 in. for attaching to the Head.

TIP OF THE NOSE

With Black

Ch 2, starting in the second ch from the hook sc [1]

Fasten off the yarn, leaving a short tail of around 4 in. for attaching to the Nose.

TOOTH

With White

Ch 3, sl st in the third ch from the hook [1]

Fasten off the yarn, leaving a tail around 20 in. long for attaching to the Mouth.

EARS (Make 2)

With Mushroom, make a magic ring

Rnd 1. Sc 6 in ring [6]

Rnd 2. (Sc 3 in the same st, inc, sc) x2 [12]

Rnd 3. Sc, (inc) x3, sc 3, (inc) x3, sc 2 [18]

Rnd 4. Sc, (sc, inc) x3, sc 3, (sc, inc) x3, sc 2 [24]

Rnd 5. Sc, (sc, dec) x3, sc 3, (sc, dec) x3, sc 2 [18]

Rnd 6. Sc in each st around [18]

Rnd 7. Sc, (dec) x3, sc 3, (dec) x3, sc 2 [12]

Rnd 8. Sc in each st around [12]

Rnd 9. (Sc, dec) x4 [8]

Rnd 10. Sc 2, press the previous rnd together so the st line up and sc them together [4]

Fasten off the yarn, leaving a short tail of around 8-10 in. for attaching to the Head.

LEGS (Make 2)

With Espresso, make a magic ring

Rnd 1. Sc 6 in ring [6]

Rnd 2. (Sc 3 in the same st, inc, sc) x2 [12]

Rnd 3. Sc, (inc) x3, sc 3, (inc) x3, sc 2 [18]

Rnd 4. Sc in each st around [18]

Rnd 5. (Dec) x4, sc 10 [14]

Rnd 6. (Dec) x2, sc 10 [12]

Rnd 7. (Sc, dec) x4 [8]

Rnds 8–13. Sc in each st around, *after a few rnds, add a small amount of stuffing to the feet* [6 rnds of 8 st]

Rnd 14. (Sc, inc) x4 [12]

Rnd 15. (Sc, inc) x6 [18]

Rnds 16–17. Sc in each st around [2 rnds of 18 st]

Rnd 18. (Sc, dec) x6 [12]

Rnd 19. Sc in each st around [12]

Rnd 20. (Dec) x6 [6]

Fasten off the yarn, leaving a short tail around 8-10 in. long. Use your needle to weave the tail through the front loops of the last rnd and pull tight to close. Set aside for now.

TAIL

With Espresso

Ch 15, starting in the second ch from the hook sl st 5, sc 5, hdc 4 [14]

Fasten off the yarn, leaving a short tail of around 8-10 in. for attaching to the Body.

JACKET

Row 1. In Varsity Red Ch 31, starting in the back bump of the second ch from the hook sc 30 in the back bumps of the ch, ch 1 and turn [30]

Rows 2–7. Sc in each st across, ch 1 and turn [6 rows of 30 st]

Row 8. Sc 3, ch 6, skip 6 st, sc 12, ch 6, skip 6 st, sc 3, ch 1 and turn [30 st with 2 armholes]

Row 9. Sc in each st and ch across, ch 1 and turn [30]

Row 10. (Sc2tog, sc 3) x3, (sc 3, sc2tog) x3, ch 1 and turn [24]

Row 11. (Sc2tog, sc2) x3, (sc 2, sc2tog) x3, ch 1 and turn [18]

Row 12. *Side 1*: Do not turn, continue down the side sc 8, (sc 2, ch 1, hdc 2) in the corner, in the previous st change to Black

Bottom: Continue around the bottom of the Jacket, hdc 28, in the previous st change to Varsity Red, (hdc 2, ch 1, sc 2) in the last st on the bottom

Side 2: Continue around to the other side of the Jacket sc 8, on previous st change to Black

Top: Ch 2, starting in the first stitch on the top of the Jacket hdc 18

Fasten off the yarn and weave in the ends.

JACKET SLEEVES (Make 2)

Rnd 1. Join Cream yarn to the corner of one of the armholes, sc 12 around the armhole [12]

Rnds 2–12. Sc in each st around, on the last st of rnd 12 change to Black [11 rnds of 12 st]

Rnd 13. Hdc 12

Fasten off the yarn and weave in the ends.

ASSEMBLY

1. Stuff and attach the Nose to the Head, directly above the Mouth, with the curve pointing down.

2. Attach the Eyes to the top of the Head just behind where the Nose is joined, with the safety eyes facing forward.

3. Attach the Eyelids to the tops of each Eye.

4. Attach the Ears to the back of the top of the Head on an angle, spanning rnds 3-6. Use blush to color the inside of the ears pink, or cut a small piece of pink felt and glue it in place.

5. Attach the Tip of the Nose where the Nose curves down.

6. Attach the Tooth to the underside of the Nose, about 2 st behind where the Tip of the Nose sits.

7. Attach the Legs on either side of the base of the Body, with the feet facing forward, so that the tops of the Legs meet the color change on the Body.

8. Pull the Jacket on. You may need to use your crochet hook to reach inside the sleeves and pull the Arms out.

9. Attach the Tail to the center back centered between the Legs.

10. Cut a strand of Espresso yarn around 4 in. long and use a Lark's Head knot to attach it to the top of the Head. Unwind the fibers of the yarn and trim to the desired length.

Mahna Mahna and the Snowths!

Not much is known about this musical trio, but they took the world by storm on the very first episode of *The Muppet Show* with their iconic song. Mahna Mahna sings lead vocals, consisting mostly of his own name and some improvised scatting. The pink Snowths are synchronized in their harmonious doo-doos. We may not know what it means or why they sing it, but it sure is catchy.

FUN FACT Mahna Mahna.

Mahna Mahna

FINISHED MEASUREMENTS
Height: 11 in. / 28 cm
Width: 5 in. / 12.7 cm

YARN
Worsted weight (#4 medium) yarn, shown in Big Twist *Value* (100% acrylic, 380 yd. / 347 m per 6 oz. / 170 g skein)
Head/Arms/Legs: Eggplant
Hair: Bright Orange
Mouth: Varsity Red
Glasses: Black
Glasses: Varsity Yellow
Nose: Medium Rose

Bulky weight (#5 bulky) yarn shown in Premier *Eyelash* (100% polyester, 214 yd. / 196 m per 3.5 oz. / 100 g ball)
Body: Spicy Lime

HOOK
US F-5 / 3.75 mm hook
US G-6 / 4 mm hook

NOTIONS
• Pink felt for the tongue
• Polyester stuffing
• Tapestry needle
• Hot glue gun
• Removable stitch markers

GAUGE
Gauge is not critical for this project. Ensure your stitches are tight so the stuffing won't show through.

SPECIAL STITCHES
Back Loop Only (BLO): Work through back loop only

NOTES
The Mouth and Head are separate pieces that get crocheted together, so it is important to make them in order.

For more information on how to make Mahna Mahna, including tips, step-by-step pictures, and videos, scan this QR code!

MOUTH

With 3.75 mm hook and Varsity Red, make a magic ring

Rnd 1. Sc 6 in ring [6]

Rnd 2. (Inc) x6 [12]

Rnd 3. (Sc, inc) x6 [18]

Rnd 4. (Sc 2, inc) x6 [24]

Rnd 5. (Sc 3, inc) x6 [30]

Rnd 6. (Sc 4, inc) x6 [36]

Fasten off the yarn and set aside for now.

HEAD

With 3.75 mm hook and Eggplant, make a magic ring

Rnd 1. Sc 6 in ring [6]

Rnd 2. (Inc) x6 [12]

Rnd 3. (Sc, inc) x6 [18]

Rnd 4. (Sc 2, inc) x6 [24]

Rnd 5. (Sc 3, inc) x6 [30]

Rnd 6. (Sc 4, inc) x6 [36]

Rnd 7. (Sc 5, inc) x6 [42]

Rnds 8–12. Sc in each st around [5 rnds of 42 st]

Rnd 13. Sc 2, *grab the Mouth and line it up with the Head, wrong sides together, so the next Eggplant st lines up with the last st that was made on the Mouth: Insert hook through both the Eggplant and Varsity Red st and crochet them together* sc 18, *work the rest of the rnd in the Eggplant st* sc 22 [42]

Rnd 14. Sc 2, *work into the Varsity Red st on the bottom half of the Mouth* sc 18, *work the rest of the rnd in the Eggplant st* sc 22 [42]

Rnd 15. Sc 2, in BLO sc 18, through both loops sc 22 [42]

Rnd 16. Sc in each st around [42]

Rnd 17. (Sc 5, dec) x6 [36]

Rnd 18. (Sc 4, dec) x6 [30]

Rnd 19. (Sc 3, dec) x6 [24]

Begin stuffing the Head—add just enough stuffing so that the Head keeps its shape without causing the Mouth to bulge:

Rnd 20. (Sc 2, dec) x6 [18]

Rnd 21. (Sc, dec) x6 [12]

Rnd 22. (Dec) x6 [6]

Fasten off the yarn, leaving a short tail around 6 in. Use your yarn needle to weave the tail through the front loops of the last rnd and pull tight to close. Pull the tail to the inside of the Head and trim any excess.

NOSE

With 3.75 mm hook and Medium Rose, make a magic ring

Rnd 1. Sc 6 in ring [6]

Rnd 2. (Inc) x6 [12]

Rnd 3. (Sc, inc) x6 [18]

Rnd 4. Sc in each st around [18]

Rnd 5. (Sc, dec) x6 [12]

Fasten off the yarn, leaving a tail around 8-10 in. for attaching to the face.

EYES (Make 2)

With 3.75 mm hook and Black, make a magic ring

Rnd 1. Sc 6 in ring [6]

Rnd 2. (Sc 3 in the same st, inc, sc) x2 [12]

Rnd 3. Sc, (inc) x3, sc 3, (inc) x3, sc 2, on the last st of the rnd change to Varsity Yellow [18]

Rnd 4. Sc, (sc, inc) x3, sc 3, (sc, inc) x3, sc 2 [24]

Fasten off the yarn, leaving a tail around 8-10 in. for attaching to the face.

BODY

With 4 mm hook and Eyelash yarn in Spicy Lime, make a magic ring

Rnd 1. Sc 6 in ring [6]

Rnd 2. (Inc) x6 [12]

Rnd 3. (Sc, inc) x6 [18]

Rnd 4. (Sc 2, inc) x6 [24]

Rnd 5. (Sc 3, inc) x6 [30]

Rnd 6. (Sc 4, inc) x6 [36]

Rnd 7. (Sc 5, inc) x6 [42]

Rnds 8–23. Sc in each st around [16 rnds of 42 st]

Rnd 24. (Sc 5, dec) x6 [36]

Rnds 25–27. Sc in each st around [3 rnds of 36 st]

Rnd 28. (Sc 4, dec) x6 [30]

Rnd 29. Sc in each st around [30]

Rnd 30. (Sc 3, dec) x6 [24]

Rnd 31. Sc in each st around [24]

Fasten off the yarn, leaving a tail around 8-10 in. for attaching to the Head.

ARMS (Make 2)

With 3.75 mm hook and Eggplant, make a magic ring

Rnd 1. Sc 8 in ring [8]

Rnds 2–3. Sc in each st around [2 rnds of 8 st]

Rnd 4. (Sc 2, dec) x2 [6]

Rnds 5–16. Sc in each st around [12 rnds of 6 st]

Rnd 17. Press the previous rnd together so the st line up and sc them together [3]

Fasten off the yarn, leaving a short tail of around 8-10 in. for attaching to the Body.

LEGS (Make 2)

With 3.75 mm hook and Eggplant, make a magic ring

Rnd 1. Sc 6 in ring [6]

Rnd 2. (Sc 3 in the same st, inc, sc) x2 [12]

Rnd 3. Sc, (inc) x3, sc 3, (inc) x3, sc 2 [18]

Rnd 4. Sc in each st around [18]

Rnd 5. (Dec) x4, sc 10 [14]

Rnd 6. (Dec) x2, sc 10 [12]

Rnd 7. (Sc, dec) x4 [8]

Rnds 8–18. Sc in each st around [11 rnds of 8 st]

Rnd 19. Sc, press the previous rnd together so the st line up and sc them together [4]

Fasten off the yarn, leaving a tail around 8-10 in. for attaching to the Body.

ASSEMBLY

1. Attach the Nose to the center of the face, directly above the Mouth.

2. Attach the lower half of each piece of the Eyes directly above the Nose so that they meet in the center. Leave the top half unattached so they can stick straight up.

3. Stuff the Body and attach it to the base of the Head.

4. Stitch the Arms on either side of the Body, about 4 rnds down from the neck.

5. Stitch the Legs to the underside of the Body with the feet facing forward.

6. Cut a large number of strands of Bright Orange around 5 in. long. Using a Lark's Head knot attach them to the back half of the Head and under the chin. Unwind the fibers and trim to desired length.

7. Cut a small heart shape out of pink felt for the tongue and use a hot glue gun to attach it inside of the Mouth.

147

Snowths

FINISHED MEASUREMENTS
Height: 9 in. / 23 cm
Width: 4 in. / 10 cm

YARN
Chunky weight (#5 bulky) yarn, shown in
Premier *Eyelash* (100% polyester, 214yd. /
196 m per 3.5 oz. / 100 g skein)
Body: **Pop Pink**

Worsted weight (#4 medium) yarn, shown in
Big Twist *Value* (100% acrylic, 380 yd. /
347 m per 6 oz. / 170 g skein)
Head/Arms/Legs/Horns: Medium Rose
Eyes: White
Eyelids: Cornflower Blue
Eyelashes: Varsity Navy Blue
Mouth: Black
Lips: Varsity Yellow

HOOK
US F-5 / 3.75 mm hook
US G-6 / 4 mm hook

NOTIONS
• Pair of 10 mm plastic safety eyes
• Polyester stuffing
• Tapestry needle
• Removable stitch markers

GAUGE
Gauge is not critical for this project. Ensure
your stitches are tight so the stuffing won't
show through.

SPECIAL STITCHES
Back Loop Only (BLO): Work through back
loop only
Front Loop Only (FLO): Work through front
loop only
Picot (picot): Ch 3, sc in the back bump of the
first ch made

NOTES
The Mouth and Head are separate pieces that get
crocheted together, so it is important to make
them in order.

For more information on how to make a Snowth, including tips,
step-by-step pictures, and videos, scan this QR code!

MOUTH

With 3.75 mm hook and Black, make a magic ring

Rnd 1. Sc 6 in ring [6]

Rnd 2. (Sc 3 in the same st, inc, sc) x2 [12]

Rnd 3. Sc, (inc) x3, sc 3, (inc) x3, sc 2 [18]

Place a stitch marker in the second to last st. Fasten off the yarn and set aside for now.

HEAD

With 3.75 mm hook and Medium Rose, make a magic ring

Rnd 1. Sc 6 in ring [6]

Rnd 2. (Inc) x6 [12]

Rnd 3. (Sc, inc) x6 [18]

Rnd 4. (Sc 2, inc) x6 [24]

Rnd 5. (Sc 3, inc) x6 [30]

Rnd 6. (Sc 4, inc) x6 [36]

Rnd 7. (Sc 5, inc) x6 [42]

Rnds 8–11. Sc in each st around [4 rnds of 42 st]

Rnd 12. (Sc 5, dec) x6 [36]

Rnds 13–16. Sc in each st around [4 rnds of 36 st]

Rnd 17. (Sc 4, dec) x6 [30]

Rnds 18–21. Sc in each st around [4 rnds of 30 st]

Rnd 22. (Sc 3, dec) x6 [24]

Rnds 23–26. Sc in each st around [4 rnds of 24 st]

Rnd 27. Sc 1, (sc, dec) x3, sc 3, (sc, dec) x3, sc 2, on the last st of rnd change to Varsity Yellow [18]

Stuff the Head fully.

Rnd 27. *Grab the Mouth and line it up with the Head, wrong sides together, so that the next st on the Head lines up with the marked st on the Mouth, and insert your hook through both st* (Inc) x 18 [36]

Fasten off the yarn and weave in the ends.

EYES (Make 2)

With 3.75 mm hook and White, make a magic ring

Rnd 1. Sc 6 in ring [6]

Rnd 2. (Inc) x6 [12]

Rnds 3–5. Sc in each st around [3 rnds of 12 st]

Insert safety eyes between rnds 3 and 4.

Fasten off the yarn, leaving a tail around 8-10 in. for attaching to the Head.

EYELIDS (Make 1 Right and 1 Left)

With 3.75 mm hook

Row 1. In Medium Rose ch 2, sc 3 in the second ch from the hook, ch 1 and turn [3]

Row 2. (Inc) x3, ch 1 and turn [6]

Row 3. (Sc, inc) x3, ch 1 and turn [9]

Row 4. (Sc 2, inc) x3, on the last st of the row change to Cornflower Blue, ch 1 and turn [12]

Rows 5-6. Sc in each st across, on the last st of row 5 change to Varsity Navy Blue, ch 1 and turn [2 rows of 12 st]

Row 7. Sc in each st across [12]

Row 8. *Snowth's Right Eyelid:* (Picot, skip 1 st, in FLO sl st) x4

Snowth's Left Eyelid: (Picot, skip 1 st, in BLO sl st) x4

Fasten off each color of yarn, leaving a short tail of around 8-10 in. of each color for attaching to the Head.

HORNS (Make 2)

With 3.75 mm hook and Medium Rose, make a magic ring

Rnd 1. Sc 6 in ring [6]

Rnd 2. Sc in each st around [6]

Rnd 3. Sc 2, (inc) x2, sc 2 [8]

Rnd 4. Sc in each st around [8]

Rnd 5. Sc 3, (inc) x2, sc 3 [10]

Rnds 6–7. Sc in each st around [2 rnds of 10 st]

Rnd 8. Sc, hdc 5, in BLO sl st 4 [10]

Rnd 9. In BLO sl st, sc 5, sc 5 in front loops from previous rnd [10]

Rnd 10. Sc in front loop from previous rnd, hdc 5, in BLO sl st 4 [10]

Rnd 11. In BLO sl st, sc 5, sc 5 in front loops from previous rnd [10]

Fasten off the yarn, leaving a tail around 8-10 in. for attaching to the Head.

BODY

With 4 mm hook and Pop Pink, make a magic ring

Rnd 1. Sc 6 in ring [6]

Rnd 2. (Inc) x6 [12]

Rnd 3. (Sc, inc) x6 [18]

Rnd 4. (Sc 2, inc) x6 [24]

Rnd 5. (Sc 3, inc) x6 [30]

Rnd 6. (Sc 4, inc) x6 [36]

Rnd 7. (Sc 5, inc) x6 [42]

Rnds 8–23. Sc in each st around [16 rnds of 42 st]

Rnd 24. (Sc 5, dec) x6 [36]

Rnds 25–27. Sc in each st around [3 rnds of 36 st]

Rnd 28. (Sc 4, dec) x6 [30]

Rnd 29. Sc in each st around [30]

Rnd 30. (Sc 3, dec) x6 [24]

Rnd 31. Sc in each st around [24]

Fasten off the yarn, leaving a tail around 8-10 in. for attaching to the Head.

ARMS (Make 2)

With 3.75 mm hook and Medium Rose, make a magic ring

Rnd 1. Sc 8 in ring [8]

Rnds 2–3. Sc in each st around [2 rnds of 8 st]

Rnd 4. (Sc 2, dec) x2 [6]

Rnds 5–16. Sc in each st around [12 rnds of 6 st]

Rnd 17. Press the previous rnd together so the st line up and sc them together [3]

Fasten off the yarn, leaving a short tail of around 8-10 in. for attaching to the Body.

LEGS (Make 2)

With 3.75 mm hook and Medium Rose make a magic ring

Rnd 1. Sc 6 in ring [6]

Rnd 2. (Sc 3 in the same st, inc, sc) x2 [12]

Rnd 3. Sc, (inc) x3, sc 3, (inc) x3, sc 2 [18]

Rnd 4. Sc in each st around [18]

Rnd 5. (Dec) x4, sc 10 [14]

Rnd 6. (Dec) x2, sc 10 [12]

Rnd 7. (Sc, dec) x4 [8]

Rnds 8–18. Sc in each st around [11 rnds of 8 st]

Rnd 19. Sc, press the previous rnd together so the st line up and sc them together [4]

Fasten off the yarn, leaving a tail around 8-10 in. for attaching to the Body.

ASSEMBLY

1. Attach the Eyes to the top of the Head, around rnds 11-13, with the safety eyes facing forward.

2. Starting with the Varsity Navy Blue tail, attach the Eyelid to the Eye, about 2 rnds up from the safety eye, so the back of the Eyelid touches the Head, and the 4 picot eyelashes are to the outside; weave in the ends. Use the Medium Rose tail to stitch the back of the Eyelid to the Head, around the Eye, weave in the ends.

3. Stuff and attach the Horns to the back of the Head, in line with the center of the magic ring, and the curve of the Horns pointing up.

4. Stuff the Body and attach it to the base of the Head.

5. Stitch the Arms on either side of the Body, about 4 rnds down from the neck.

6. Stitch the Legs to the underside of the Body with the feet facing forward.

The Swedish Chef!

Whether wielding a mallet or clutching a cleaver, the Swedish Chef is a master of mayhem in the kitchen. Chef may not make great meals, but he wages a never-ending battle with the fruits, vegetables, cheeses, lobsters, and other assorted Muppet foods. He is a blur of motion in the kitchen, where he chops, pounds, clobbers, and otherwise tries to subdue his always uncooperative ingredients. Chef speaks a dialect known as Møck Swedish. No one is absolutely sure what he's saying.

FUN FACT The Swedish Chef serves meatballs with a tennis racquet.

The Swedish Chef

FINISHED MEASUREMENTS

Height: 10 in. / 25.5 cm
Width: 4.5 in. / 11.5 cm

YARN

Worsted weight (#4 medium) yarn, shown in Big Twist *Value* (100% acrylic, 380 yd. / 347 m per 6 oz. / 170 g skein)

Head/Body: Cream
Nose: Cosmetic Pink
Shirt: Cornflower Blue
Pants: Denim
Shoes: Black
Hair: Toffee
Apron/Hat: White
Bow Tie: Magenta

HOOK

US F-5 / 3.75 mm hook

NOTIONS

• Polyester stuffing
• Tapestry needle
• Pet brush or comb
• Removable stitch markers

GAUGE

Gauge is not critical for this project. Ensure your stitches are tight so the stuffing won't show through

SPECIAL STITCHES

Pop3: Popcorn stitch with 3 double crochet stitches
Sc2tog: Single crochet 2 stitches together

For more information on how to make Swedish Chef, including tips, step-by-step pictures, and videos, scan this QR code!

https://www.drewbieszoo.com/muppets-swedish-chef-979-8-88674-177-3

ARMS (Make 2)

With Cream, make a magic ring

Rnd 1. Sc 6 in ring [6]

Rnd 2. (Inc) x6 [12]

Rnd 3. (Sc 2, inc) x4 [16]

Rnd 4. Sc in each st around [16]

Rnd 5. Sc, pop3, sc 14 [16]

Rnd 6. (Sc 2, dec) x 4, on the last st of the rnd change to Cornflower Blue [12]

Rnds 7–20. Sc in each st around [14 rnds of 12 st]

Rnd 21. Sc 5 (to get the proper alignment), press the previous rnd together so the st line up and sc them together [6]

Fasten off the yarn and weave in the ends.

HEAD AND BODY

With Cream, make a magic ring

Rnd 1. Sc 6 in ring [6]

Rnd 2. (Inc) x6 [12]

Rnd 3. (Sc, inc) x6 [18]

Rnd 4. (Sc 2, inc) x6 [24]

Rnd 5. (Sc 3, inc) x6 [30]

Rnds 6–8. Sc in each st around [3 rnds of 30 st]

Rnd 9. (Sc 4, inc) x6 [36]

Rnd 10. (Sc 5, inc) x6 [42]

Rnds 11–13. Sc in each st around [3 rnds of 42 st]

Rnd 14. (Sc 5, dec) x6 [36]

Rnd 15. (Sc 4, dec) x6 [30]

Begin stuffing the Head fully, continue stuffing as you go:

Rnd 16. (Sc 3, dec) x6 [24]

Rnd 17. (Sc 2, dec) x6 [18]

Rnd 18. (Sc, dec) x6, on the last st of the rnd change to Cornflower Blue [12]

Rnd 19. (Sc, inc) x6 [18]

Rnd 20. (Sc 2, inc) x6 [24]

Rnd 21. (Sc 3, inc) x6 [30]

Rnd 22. *Grab one of the Arms and place it so the 6 st at the top line up with the next 6 st on the body and sc them together*, sc 9, *grab the other Arm and attach in the same manner as the first*, sc 9 [30 st with 2 arms]

Rnd 23. Sc in each st around [30]

Rnd 24. (Sc 4, inc) x6 [36]

Rnds 25–26. Sc in each st around [2 rnds of 36 st]

Rnd 27. (Sc 5, inc) x6 [42]

Rnds 28–30. Sc in each st around, on the last st of rnd 30 change to Denim yarn [3 rnds of 42 st]

Rnds 31–32. Sc in each st around [2 rnds of 42 st]

Rnd 33. (Sc 5, dec) x6 [36]

Rnd 34. (Sc 4, dec) x6 [30]

Begin stuffing the Body fully and continue stuffing as you go.

Rnd 35. (Sc 3, dec) x6 [24]

Rnd 36. (Sc 2, dec) x6 [18]

Rnd 37. (Sc, dec) x6 [12]

Rnd 38. (Dec) x6 [6]

Fasten off the yarn, leaving a short tail around 6 in. Use your needle to weave the tail through the front loops of the last rnd and pull tight to close. Pull the tail to the inside of the Body and trim any excess.

CHEF'S HAT

With White, make a magic ring

Rnd 1. Sc 6 in ring [6]

Rnd 2. (Inc) x6 [12]

Rnd 3. (Sc, inc) x6 [18]

Rnd 4. (Sc 2, inc) x6 [24]

Rnd 5. (Sc 3, inc) x6 [30]

Rnd 6. (Sc 4, inc) x6 [36]

Rnd 7. (Sc 5, inc) x6 [42]

Rnd 8. (Sc 6, inc) x6 [48]

Rnd 9. In BLO sc in each back loop around [48]

Rnds 10–12. Sc in each st around [3 rnds of 48 st]

Rnd 13. (Sc 6, dec) x6 [42]

Rnd 14. (Sc 5, dec) x6 [36]

Rnd 15. (Sc 4, dec) x6 [30]

Rnd 16. (Sc 3, dec) x6 [24]

Rnd 17. In BLO sc in each back loop around [24]

Rnds 18–20. Sc in each st around [3 rnds of 24 st]

Fasten off the yarn, leaving a short tail of around 8-10 in. for attaching to the Head.

NOSE

With Cosmetic Pink, make a magic ring

Rnd 1. Sc 6 in ring [6]

Rnd 2. Sc 3 in the same st, sc 5 [8]

Rnd 3. Sc 1, sc-ch 2-sc in the same st, sc 6 [9]

Fasten off the yarn, leaving a short tail of around 8-10 in. for attaching to the Head.

LOWER LIP

With Cream

Row 1. Ch 6, starting in the second ch from the hook sc 4, sc 3 in the same st, continue to the other side of the ch, skip 1 st, sc 3, sc 3 in the same st [13]

Row 2. Sc in each st around [13]

Row 3. Press the previous rnd together so the st line up, skip 1 st, and sc them together [7]

Fasten off the yarn, leaving a short tail of around 8-10 in. for attaching to the Head.

LEGS (Make 2)

With Black, make a magic ring

Rnd 1. Sc 6 in ring [6]

Rnd 2. (Sc 3 in the same st, inc, sc) x2 [12]

Rnd 3. Sc, (inc) x3, sc 3, (inc) x3, sc 2 [18]

Rnd 4. Sc 1, (sc, inc) x3, sc 3, (sc, inc) x3, sc 2 [24]

Rnds 5–6. Sc in each st around [2 rnds of 24 st]

Rnd 7. Sc, (dec) x6, sc 11 [18]

Rnd 8. Sc in each st around, on the last st of the rnd change to Denim [18]

Rnds 9–11. Sc in each st around [3 rnds of 18 st]

Add stuffing to the foot and partially up the Leg; the rest of the Leg remains unstuffed:

Rnd 12. (Sc 4, dec) x3 [15]

Rnds 13–15. Sc in each st around [3 rnds of 15 st]

Rnd 16. (Sc 3, dec) x3 [12]

Rnds 17–18. Sc in each st around [2 rnds of 12 st]

Rnd 19. Sc, press the previous rnd together so the st line up and sc them together [6]

Fasten off the yarn, leaving a short tail of around 8-10 in. for attaching to the Body.

BOW TIE

With Magenta, make a magic ring

Row 1. Ch 7, dc in the third ch from the hook, sc, sl st, sc, dc 2 in the same st.

Fasten off the yarn, leaving a medium length tail around 12-14 in. for attaching to the Body.

APRON

With White

Row 1. Ch 19, starting in the back bump of the second ch from the hook sc 18, ch 1 and turn [18]

Rows 2–12. Sc in each st across, ch 1 and turn [11 rows of 18 st]

Row 13. Sc2tog, sc 14, sc2tog, ch 1 and turn [16]

Row 14. Sc2tog, sc 12, sc2tog, ch 1 and turn [14]

Row 15. Sc2tog, sc 10, sc2tog, ch 1 and turn [12]

Row 16. Sc2tog, sc 8, sc2tog, ch 1 and turn [10]

Row 17. Sc2tog, sc 6, sc2tog, ch 1 and turn [8]

Rows 18–20. Sc in each st across, ch 1 and turn (do not ch after row 20) [3 rows of 8 st]

Row 21. *Neck:* Ch 20, making sure the ch is not twisted, place the Apron on the Body and bring the ch around the back of the neck and continue down the other side of the Apron

Side 1: Sc 7 (which should bring you to the widest point of the Apron. If you come up short or have gone too far, adjust the number of st so you end up at the corner). Ch 25, starting in the second ch from the hook, sl st 24, sc 11 down the side, (sc, ch 1, sc) in the bottom corner

Bottom: Continue along the bottom of the Apron, sc 17, (sc, ch 1, sc) in the other bottom corner

Side 2: Continue up the other side of the Apron, sc 11 (or however many st it takes to get you to the corner where it begins to narrow). Ch 25, starting in the second ch from the hook, sl st 24, sc 7 back to the top corner of the Apron

Top: Sc 20 in the back bumps of the chain that goes around the back of the neck.

Fasten off the yarn and weave in the ends.

ASSEMBLY

1. Stitch the Nose to the center of the face, spanning rnds 7-11, with the point facing up. When you have stitched part of the Nose down, add a little stuffing to the bottom portion of the Nose, then finish attaching it.

2. Stitch the bottom edge of the Lower Lip 3 rnds up from the color change at the neck.

3. *Chef's left Ear*: join Cream yarn to the side of the Head, between rnds 12 and 13, dc 3 in the same space 2 rnds up, sl st 1 rnd up. Fasten off the yarn and weave in the ends.

Chef's right Ear: join Cream yarn to the side of the Head, between rnds 9 and 10, dc 3 in the same space 2 rnds down, sl st 1 rnd down. Fasten off the yarn and weave in the ends.

4. Grab the Bow Tie and weave in the shorter tail, weave the longer tail to the center of the Bow Tie. Make a vertical stitch 2 rnds tall at the top center of the shirt, catching the middle of the Tie. Make multiple passes in the same direction to build up the "knot" of the Bow Tie.

5. Attach the top of the Legs to the bottom of the Body so that they meet in the center; make sure the feet are facing forward.

6. With the Apron in front, tie the Apron strings in the back.

7. Without stuffing, attach the base of the Chef's Hat to the top of the Head. Play around with the top portion of the hat until it looks how you would like it to.

8. Cut a large number of strands of Toffee around 3 in. long. Using a Lark's Head Knot attach the strands to the Head. Attach 2 strands at once to give a fuller look. (When attaching the strands be sure that your hook is always pointed to the bottom of the body when first inserted. This will ensure that the knot is hidden.)

Hair: Attach a straight line of strands at the base of Chef's Hat, starting and ending just behind the Ears.

Eyebrows: Attach 4 groups of 2 strands per eyebrow, with one st in between. The sides of the eyebrows nearest to the Nose should touch the base of the Chef's Hat, and curve down the face as they move away from the Nose.

Mustache: Attach the strands in a straight line directly below the Nose, typically around 9 groups of 2 strands.

9. Use a pet brush or comb to brush out all of the strands. For the hair, less brushing is better, to keep some of the natural waves of the yarn fiber. You can always brush more, but you can't brush less. After you've achieved your desired texture, trim the hair to suit your taste.

Hair: Around .5-.75 in. long

Eyebrows: Around .25-.5 in. long

Mustache: Around .5 in. toward the center, but gradually getting longer as you move away from the Nose, around .75 in. at the longest.

ROLL THE CREDITS (AND RESOURCES)!

TIPS, TRICKS, AND TECHNIQUES FOR CREATING YOUR MUPPET

GET THE LOOK: CHOOSING YOUR HOOK

Most of the patterns in this book were made using a US F-5/3.75 mm or US G-6/4.00 mm hook; however, you may need to adjust which size hook you choose depending on factors like your choice of yarn and the tension with which you crochet. I always recommend working up a sample swatch when trying new yarn to see which hook you should use.

Your hook should be able to slide easily into the next stitch without too much resistance. If your stitches are too tight it may mean that you are using a hook that is too small, and you may want to go up a hook size. On the other hand, if there are large gaps in between stitches, you may be using a hook that is too large and you may want to go down a hook size.

US	METRIC
B-1	2.25 mm
C-2	2.75 mm
D-3	3.25 mm
E-4	3.50 mm
F-5	3.75 mm
G-6	4.00 mm
7	4.50 mm
H-8	5.00 mm
I-9	5.50 mm
J-10	6.00 mm
K-10.5	6.50 mm
L-11	8.00 mm
M-13	9.00 mm
N-15	10.00 mm
P-16	12.00 mm

YOU'VE GOT ME IN STITCHES! TIPS FOR SEWING

While many of the patterns in this book have elements that can be crocheted together, they all require a fair bit of sewing as well. Sewing crochet pieces together can be tricky and can have a massive impact on the final result, so it's important to set yourself up for success.

For smaller pieces, use U-pins to hold the piece in place while you sew. Larger pieces can be held in place by hand or with a long, thin knitting needle.

When sewing, try to insert your tapestry needle into the spaces between stitches rather than through the center. This will give a much cleaner finish.

STUFFING: IT'S SO FULL-FILLING

For most pieces, I recommend stuffing them as fully as you can without having the filling show through between the stitches. Polyester stuffing has a tendency to settle over time, and stuffing firmly will keep your Muppets from looking deflated later on. Stuffing will also play a large role in the final shape of your piece, so here are a few tips to help your Muppets look their best:

Tear the stuffing into smaller pieces rather than trying to stuff a big piece in all at once. This will help keep it from looking clumpy.

Make sure the stuffing reaches into all of the corners and edges, so the piece will maintain the correct shape.

For smaller or narrower pieces, use the back end of your crochet hook or a chopstick to push small amounts of stuffing where they need to go.

Many of The Muppets have open mouths so their heads may be a bit tricky to stuff. You want to add enough stuffing above and below the mouth on the inside of the head so the head will maintain its shape but not so much stuffing that the mouth bulges out. It may be helpful to hold the Muppet's head as if it is biting your finger while you stuff. This makes sure that you aren't over-stuffing.

TO SEW OR NOT TO SEW? CROCHETING PIECES TOGETHER

Many of the patterns in this book involve crocheting pieces together: mouths get crocheted onto heads, arms get attached, etc. If necessary, the pattern will give specific information as to how to line up these pieces. Typically, the pieces will either be held with the wrong sides (insides) together or the right sides (outsides) together. If it's a piece like an arm, it may be directional like "thumbs facing toward the front of the body." Be sure to crochet the pieces in the correct order so that you'll be able to attach them at the appropriate time.

THINGS ARE GETTING FUZZY: BRUSHING OUT YOUR YARN

Some of The Muppets in this book, like Sam Eagle and Beaker, will need to be a bit fluffy in areas. This is achieved by brushing the fibers of the yarn back to its fuzzy roots. The easiest way to do this is by using a pet slicker brush (one with many thin wire bristles). All of the yarn that will be brushed out has been attached using a Lark's Head knot. If using standard worsted weight yarn, it will most likely be plied, meaning that the yarn is composed of several strands twisted together. I find it easier to separate each strand of yarn into its individual plies before brushing, to get the smoothest result.

HEARTFELT FELT DETAILS

Felt is a wonderful addition to many amigurumi pieces. It can be used to make details that would be too bulky if they were made out of yarn. I recommend getting sheets of craft felt from your local craft supply store, in the colors you'll need. I like to cut all my felt details by hand, before either using a hot glue gun to attach them, or if I'm feeling extra tedious, I will use an embroidery needle and embroidery floss to sew them in place.

FOR MORE TIPS, TRICKS, AND TECHNIQUES

Scan this QR code for more instructions, videos, and other handy tips and content!

STITCH ABBREVIATIONS

Ch: Chain
Sc: Single crochet
Hdc: Half double crochet
Dc: Double crochet
Sl st: Slip stitch
BLO: Back loop only
FLO: Front loop only
Pop[x]: Popcorn stitch, x = the number of dc to be made in the same st
Inc: Increase
Dec: Invisible decrease
Sc2tog: Sc 2 st together
St: Stitch/stiches
Rnd: Round

US VS. UK TERMS

This book is written using US terminology. If you are more familiar with UK terms, here is a helpful conversion chart:

US TERMS	UK TERMS
Sl st— slip stitch	Ss—slip stitch
Sc—single crochet	Dc—double crochet
Hdc—half double crochet	Htc—half treble crochet
Dc—double crochet	Tc—treble crochet
Sc2tog—single crochet 2 stitches together	Dc2tog—double crochet 2 stitches together

GLOSSARY OF STITCHES AND TECHNIQUES

SLIP KNOT

Make a loop with the yarn. Insert your index finger and thumb through the loop and grab the working yarn (connected to the skein) and pull it through the loop, holding on to the tail. Pull until a knot is formed, insert your hook through the new loop and pull the working yarn to tighten the knot.

CHAIN

With a slip knot on your hook, yarn over and pull up a loop through the slip knot. Yarn over and pull up a loop through the loop on your hook. Repeat these steps as many times as the pattern calls for.

BACK BUMP OF CHAIN

A chain consists of two loops in the front and a small bump on the back. Typically, when working into the chain you will work through one of the loops on the front side, but for certain pieces in this book, you will want to work through the small bump on the back of the chain instead.

MAGIC RING

Make a loop with the yarn, leaving a tail around 4 in. long. Insert your hook into the loop and while holding the loop steady, pull the working yarn through. Keep the working yarn loose while using your hook to grab the working yarn on the other side of the loop and pull it through the loop on your hook. Single crochet into the ring by inserting your hook through the large loop, yarn over and pull the working yarn through, yarn over and pull through both loops on the hook. Single crochet the number of stitches the pattern calls for into the magic ring and then pull the tail tight to close the ring. (If you do not like this method, you can also chain 2 and work the number of single crochet the pattern calls for into the second chain from the hook.)

SINGLE CROCHET

Insert your hook through both loops of the next stitch, yarn over and pull the working yarn through the stitch (2 loops on the hook), yarn over and pull the working yarn through both loops on the hook.

HALF DOUBLE CROCHET

Yarn over, insert your hook through both loops of the next stitch, yarn over and pull the working yarn through the stitch (3 loops on the hook), yarn over and pull the working yarn through all 3 loops on the hook.

DOUBLE CROCHET

Yarn over, insert your hook through both loops of the next stitch, yarn over and pull the working yarn through the stitch (3 loops on the hook), yarn over and pull the working yarn through the first 2 loops on the hook (2 loops on the hook), yarn over and pull the working yarn through both loops on the hook.

SLIP STITCH

Insert your hook through both loops of the next stitch, yarn over and pull the working yarn through the stitch and through the loop on the hook.

BACK LOOP ONLY

Work in the back loop of the stitch only: the loop that is furthest from you.

FRONT LOOP ONLY

Work in the front loop of the stitch only: the loop that is closest to you.

PICOT

There are many ways to make a picot. For this book they are worked as follows:
1. Chain 3
2. Single crochet into the back bump of the third chain from the hook

POPCORN STITCH

The popcorn stitch is traditionally made with 5 double crochet in the same stitch, then the hook is removed from the working loop, inserted through both loops of the first double crochet made and back through the working loop, the working loop is then pulled through the first double crochet made to form a small bump. The patterns in this book use variations of the popcorn stitch with different numbers of double crochet worked into the same stitch.

INCREASE

Make 2 single crochet in the same stitch to increase the number of stitches by 1.

HALF DOUBLE CROCHET INCREASE

Make 2 half double crochet in the same stitch to increase the number of stitches by 1.

INVISIBLE DECREASE

Insert hook through the front loops of the next 2 stitches, yarn over and pull the working yarn through both front loops (2 loops on the hook), yarn over and pull the working yarn through both loops on the hook (crocheting 2 stitches together to decrease the number of stitches by 1).

SINGLE CROCHET 2 STITCHES TOGETHER (SC2TOG)

Insert hook through both loops of the next stitch, yarn over and pull the working yarn through the stitch (2 loops on the hook), insert hook through both loops of the following stitch, yarn over and pull the working yarn through the stitch (3 loops on the hook), yarn over and pull the working yarn through all 3 loops on the hook (crocheting 2 stitches together to decrease the number of stitches by 1).

LARK'S HEAD KNOT

Used to attach short strands of yarn to a finished piece. Insert your hook in and out under the desired stitch on your piece, use the hook to grab the middle of the strand of yarn and pull up a small loop (leaving 2 short yarn tails on the other side of the stitch), use the hook to pull the 2 short yarn tails through the small loop. Pull the yarn tails to tighten the Lark's Head knot.

COLOR CHANGE

Color changes occur on the last stitch before the desired color will be used. Work the stitch in the old color until 2 loops remain on the hook, then use your hook to pull a loop of the new color through both loops. Tie the tail of the new color to the working yarn of the old color and cut the old color. If the color change occurs on the inside of a piece that will be stuffed there is no need to weave in the ends. If the color change occurs on a piece where the wrong side will be visible (Scooter's Jacket for example) then weave in the ends securely.

RIGHT SIDE

When crocheting in the round, the right side is the outside of your project. If you are right-handed, you will be working counterclockwise, if you are left-handed, you will be working clockwise.

WRONG SIDE

When crocheting in the round, the wrong side is the inside of your project. You will know if you are working with the wrong side out if you are right-handed and you are working clockwise, or if you are left-handed and you are working counterclockwise. The patterns in this book are all written with the right side facing out; if you are working with the wrong side out, you will want to turn the piece so that it is right side out.

WEAVING IN ENDS

For pieces that are stuffed, you'll simply have to use your hook to pull the ends to the inside of the piece. For pieces that are not stuffed, you will need to use your tapestry needle to work the ends back and forth through the nearby stitches to secure them in place before trimming them.

ACKNOWLEDGMENTS

An impossibly large thank you to my editor, Karyn Gerhard, for your enthusiasm, encouragement, and for holding my hand through every step of this process.

Thank you to BJ Berti for the excellent technical editing, and to everyone at Weldon Owen and Insight Editions who played a role in bringing this book into being.

A special thank you to Dani Iglesias from The Muppets Studio for her attention to detail and for inspiring some of my best work.

Words cannot express my gratitude to the wonderful women in my Book Chat for keeping me sane as I worked late into the night (and morning). Thank you to the Brochet Boys, the Quilting Queens, and my NY crochet retreat friends for all of the love and encouragement.

A million thanks to Sarah for being my emotional support human throughout this process, and all my love to the crochet community online that I'm so lucky to be a part of.

I am deeply grateful to Peggy, who knows far too much about me. The voice in my head that tells me I can do anything sounds an awful lot like you.

A special thanks to my uncle, Pete Souza, for his guidance, assistance, and support.

Lastly, thank you to my family for their eternal love and support.

ABOUT THE MUPPETS STUDIO

The Muppets are unlikely friends rising up against all odds to realize their dream: making the world a whole lot happier and a little bit weirder. From their humble beginnings on *The Muppet Show*, Kermit the Frog, Miss Piggy, Fozzie Bear, Gonzo, and the rest of the gang soared to "super-Muppetdom" in films such as *The Muppet Movie, Muppets Take Manhattan,* and *The Muppet Christmas Carol.* But they wanted to do even more! At The Muppets Studio, we share their dreams of singing, dancing, and making people happy, so we got Kermit and the gang on the phone and got busy creating all kinds of wonderful and weird content. (Wonderful and weird content just like the crochet book you're now holding!) The Muppets Studio is behind award-winning projects like the feature film *The Muppets,* the Halloween special *Muppets Haunted Mansion,* and the rockin' series *The Muppets Mayhem* for Disney+. A proud part of The Walt Disney Company, it's an honor for us to carry on the creative legacy of these beloved characters. There's no telling where The Muppets will go next, but thanks to Muppet Labs, Bunsen and Beaker have us prepared for any scientific probability . . . or improbability!

ABOUT THE AUTHOR

Drew Hill is an amigurumi designer and fiber arts enthusiast. He learned to knit at the age of ten and has been passionate about yarn ever since. At seventeen, Drew picked up a crochet hook for the first time and is now rarely seen without one. After years of crocheting as a hobby, he decided to take things to the next level and opened Drewbie's Zoo to sell finished amigurumi as well as offer both free and premium patterns.

Drew has found a wonderful home in the fiber arts community on social media, and loves sharing thoughtful, silly, and lighthearted content. He designs patterns for all sorts of amigurumi that range from easy to challenging. In 2022, he released his first book of patterns, *Crochet Magical Creatures*, which features many adorably enchanting and beginner-friendly designs.

A graduate from the University of Michigan with a BFA in Theatre Design & Production, Drew has worked as a costume designer and has found ways to sneak his fiber crafts into most productions. These days he spends his time in his craft dungeon, experimenting with new patterns. When he's not working, Drew enjoys playing with his golden retriever Billy and eating delicious vegan food.

Website: www.drewbieszoo.com
Instagram: @drewbieszoo
TikTok: @drewbies.zoo

weldon**owen**

an imprint of Insight Editions
P.O. Box 3088
San Rafael, CA 94912
www.weldonowen.com

CEO Raoul Goff
VP Publisher Roger Shaw
Editorial Director Katie Killebrew
Senior Editor Karyn Gerhard
Editorial Assistant Jon Ellis
VP Creative Chrissy Kwasnik
Art Director and Designer Allister Fein
Art Direction, Styled Photography Megan Sinead Bingham
VP Manufacturing Alix Nicholaeff
Sr. Production Manager Joshua Smith
Sr Production Manager, Subsidiary Rights Lina s Palma-Temena

Weldon Owen would also like to thank BJ Berti, Carla Kipen, and Ted Thomas
for their work on this project.

© 2024 Disney

Amigurumi photography by Lorena Masso and Ted Thomas
Character images courtesy of The Walt Disney Company

ISBN: 979-8-88674-177-3

Manufactured in China by Insight Editions
10 9 8 7 6 5 4 3 2 1

ROOTS of PEACE   REPLANTED PAPER

Insight Editions, in association with Roots of Peace, will plant two trees for each
tree used in the manufacturing of this book. Roots of Peace is an internationally
renowned humanitarian organization dedicated to eradicating land mines worldwide
and converting war-torn lands into productive farms and wildlife habitats. Roots of
Peace will plant two million fruit and nut trees in Afghanistan and provide farmers
there with the skills and support necessary for sustainable land use.